GRADING PLACES

ECONOMIC POLICY INSTITUTE

GRADING PLACES

What Do the Business Climate Rankings Really Tell Us?

Peter Fisher

ECONOMIC POLICY INSTITUTE

About the Author

Peter Fisher is a professor in the Graduate Program in Urban and Regional Planning at the University of Iowa, where he has taught since 1977. His research and teaching interests are centered on state and local government finance, economic development policy, and poverty and income inequality. He has served as a consultant on tax issues, welfare reform, and economic development policy for state government agencies, labor unions, and non-profit organizations. More recently, he has become part-time research director for the Iowa Policy Project, a state-level non-profit public policy research organization focusing on the Iowa economy and state budget and tax policy. He is the co-author, with Alan Peters, of *Industrial Incentives: Competition Among American States and Cities* (1998), and *State Enterprise Zone Programs: Have they Worked?* (2002), both published by the W.E. Upjohn Institute for Employment Research. He has also published a number of journal articles on tax incentives and economic development policy. He received a B.A. from Haverford College in 1968 and a Ph.D. in economics from the University of Wisconsin – Madison in 1978.

ECONOMIC POLICY INSTITUTE
1660 L Street, NW, Suite 1200
Washington, D.C. 20036

http://www.epi.org

ISBN: 1-932066-21-7

Table of contents

Acknowledgments

I would like to thank Michael Mazerov of the Center on Budget and Policy Priorities and Zach Schiller of Policy Matters Ohio for their very helpful review of an earlier draft of this report. I would particularly like to thank Michael Ettlinger of the Economic Policy Institute for guiding the project through to completion and for providing incisive and extensive commentary on the report that greatly improved the final product.

This research was funded by the Annie E. Casey Foundation. We thank them for their support but acknowledge that the findings and conclusions presented in this report are those of the author alone, and do not necessarily reflect the opinions of the Foundation.

Other recent books from the Economic Policy Institute

The State of Working America 2004/2005

Rethinking Growth Strategies: How State and Local Taxes and Services Affect Economic Development

Growing State Economies: How Taxes and Public Services Affect Private-Sector Performance

Exceptional Returns: Economic, Fiscal, and Social Benefits of Investment in Early Childhood Development

Smart Money: Education and Economic Development

The Charter School Dust-Up: Examining the Evidence on Enrollment and Achievement

Class and Schools: Using Social, Economic, and Educational Reform to Close the Black-White Achievement Gap

Racing To The Bottom: How Antiquated Public Policy Is Destroying the Best Jobs in Telecommunications

Amtrak Privatization: The Route to Failure

Executive summary

In the United States today, at least eight groups produce rankings of states and cities that are widely cited by public officials and businesses to make the case for changing public policy to enhance a state's prospects for growth. These rankings are based on each organization's version of an "index" that purports to show which states or cities have the best "business climate," or the most "competitive" tax and regulatory environment, or the conditions most conducive to small business growth and entrepreneurialism.

In this report we critique five major rankings that claim to measure the *capacity* or *potential* for economic growth. Are they based on science? Do they have biases? Do they in fact work as predictors of economic activity? The indices analyzed here vary widely in the factors that underlie them, but they have one thing in common: they claim that places with lower taxes and fewer government regulations are better. Many of the reports based on these rankings then draw explicit policy recommendations: cut taxes, shrink government, and reduce regulations, and your state or city will experience more business investment, more job creation, or more small business development. These policy recommendations are valid only if the index is a valid measure of the state or city's growth climate.

The indexes of competitiveness described and critiqued in detail in this report are:

- The "Small Business Survival Index," produced annually by the Small Business and Entrepreneurship Council.

- The "State Business Tax Climate Index," produced annually by the Tax Foundation.

- The "Metro Area and State Competitiveness Report," produced annually by the Beacon Hill Institute.

- The "Fiscal Policy Report Card on America's Governors," prepared biennially by the Cato Institute.

- The "Economic Freedom Index," first published by the Pacific Research Institute in 2004.

These five indexes produce widely different rankings of the states, despite the fact that all of the organizations creating these indexes assert that they are measuring something of critical importance to a state's economic future and its potential for growth. Thirty-four of the 50 states can claim that they are in the top 10 in terms of business climate or competitiveness; they just have to pick which of the five indexes they want to point to. Business interests in just about any state can find at least one ranking to support an argument for cutting business taxes to make the state more competitive. In all but eight states, one can find at least one index that puts the state in the bottom half of all states.

The underlying problem with the five indexes is twofold: none of them actually do a very good job of measuring what it is they claim to measure, and they do not, for the most part, set out to measure the right things to begin with. The Small Business Survival Index is almost entirely about tax burdens on upper-income residents rather than about state programs or policies to assist entrepreneurship or small business growth. The State Business Tax Climate Index is a large and complex undertaking but ends up generating a number that has little relation to the actual taxes falling on new business investment in a state. The Beacon Hill Competitiveness Index is a mishmash of causal and performance variables that render it useless as an overall predictor of anything. The Cato Institute's Fiscal Policy Report Card is little more than a rating of governors on their aggressiveness in promoting an agenda of limited government. And the Economic Freedom Index is a sometimes bizarre collection of policies and laws libertarians love, or love to hate, but few have any plausible connection to a state's economic potential.

Do the businesses making investment and location decisions pay any attention to these state rankings? A look at the publications aimed at corporate location executives and site location consultants suggest that they do not. Current rankings conducted by business magazines tend to be much broader in scope. The two that are aimed at creating an index of growth potential or competitiveness look at the whole range of factors that are important to business and/or to employees, including labor costs, cultural and recreational amenities, climate, energy costs, transportation, educational attainment, school quality, and health care. Tax levels are part of the equation, but only a small part.

It is precisely because the competitiveness indexes produced by the ideological think tanks are aimed at promoting particular kinds of legislation that they do a poor job of predicting state economic growth: the measures used must pass an ideology screen, so the validity and relevance criteria go by the wayside. This is also why these rankings are ignored by the business people actually making the decisions. They should be ignored by policy makers for the same reason.

Introduction

Newspapers love rankings. Their readers have an apparently insatiable interest in how a particular state or city compares to others. Recognizing this, a number of advocacy think tanks have accommodated the press in recent years by creating and publicizing rankings that purport to show which states or cities have the best "business climate," the most "competitive" tax and regulatory environment, or the conditions most conducive to small business growth and entrepreneurialism.

These rankings are based on each organization's version of an "index" that is supposed to summarize the various factors that make a place more competitive or conducive to economic growth. The purpose of this report is to dissect these various indices to see what really drives them. Are they based on science? Do they have biases? Do they in fact work as predictors of economic activity?

Competitiveness rankings date back to the 1970s, when a so-called "economic war between the states" was heating up. In 1979, the accounting firm Grant Thornton began to produce an annual ranking of the states based on their business climates. In the ensuing decade, the "Grant Thornton Index" gained considerable publicity and was widely cited by public officials and businesses to make the case for changing public policy to enhance a state's prospects for growth. But in 1986 it was harshly criticized in a report by the Corporation for Enterprise Development for its methodology and its bias in favor of certain kinds of policies (CFED 1986). In the face of this and other criticism, the index was abandoned a few years later.

It didn't take long for the void to be filled: at least eight groups now produce rankings of states or cities on a regular basis. In this report we critique in detail five rankings that claim to measure the *capacity* or *potential* for economic growth. The indices analyzed here vary widely in the factors that underlie them, but they have one thing in common: they claim that places with lower taxes and fewer government regulations are better. The reports based on these rankings then draw explicit policy recommendations: cut taxes, shrink government, and reduce regulations, and your state or city will experience more business investment, more job creation, or more small business development.

These policy recommendations are valid only if the index is a valid measure of the state or city's growth climate. That is the issue investigated in this report. For each index we ask a series of questions aimed at assessing the validity of its components and the way in which the components are combined.

The first question is: does the index include all of the relevant variables, and only relevant variables? For example, an index may purport to measure the capacity for growth, but are the major factors that research has shown to contribute to growth included in the index? Does the index include factors that are not plausibly related to growth? An index could be called "The Best State Economic Policy Index," but if the ranking is determined by the number of letters in the state's name, or other implausible factors, it will not be informative about which states have the best economic policies.

Just as bad, an index that purports to measure the *climate* for growth may include indicators of the state's actual performance, such as new business starts or growth in per capita income. Creating a multidimensional measure of state economic performance may well be a useful thing, but including performance measures in a supposedly causal index, and then showing that the index predicts performance, is circular reasoning.

The second question that should be asked of an index is: do the causal variables in fact measure what they claim to measure? For example, a sub-index might be labeled "business tax burden." This may be a legitimate thing to include in a causal index, but only if the business tax burden is measured appropriately.

The third question is: how does the index deal with the problem of combining disparate measures into a single index number? For example, if one believed the only important factors in economic growth were the state corporate income tax rate and state per-capita personal health care expenditures, how would one construct an index? To start with, corporate income tax rates are expressed as a percentage, with all rates under 10%, and health care expenditures range from approximately $3,000 to $7,000. If these were just added together for each state the index would really only measure the health care expenditures because the numbers and range are so much greater than for the corporate income tax. The index components should be converted to a similar scale before they are combined.

Combining disparate measures also entails explicit or implicit weighting. Even if the corporate income tax and health expenditures are scaled so that one does not dominate the other in the index, the question remains as to whether one is more important than the other as a cause of economic growth. An index might weight components according to their assumed importance, and one sure sign of an index that isn't serious is that it weights all its components the same. We know that every factor is not of equal importance in causing economic growth, and a failure to appropriately weight factors is a sign of a failed index. (Appendix D contains a more complete discussion of the issues involved in combining factors to create an index.)

Finally, does the index do a good job of predicting why some states or cities grew more rapidly than others over some time period? In other words, an index can be put to the test, and this study does just that. It uses simple statistical models to evaluate whether there is a connection between competitiveness and business climate index rankings and actual economic performance.

These questions raise a broader one: is there a "right way" to measure what these indexes purport to measure? Are these indexes legitimate tools? Is there a science of evaluating competitiveness and business climate? There is indeed a science—it is called the statistical analysis of factors contributing to state or metro area growth. A large body of scholarly research has focused on this question, and the methodology used is generally some form of multiple regression analysis. The explanatory variables in these models are like the individual measures that go into the making of an index.

The key difference between an index and a statistical model is that in a statistical analysis the variables are not weighted arbitrarily, as they are in an index. Instead, the weights are produced by the statistical tools used in the analysis. Each weight (or regression coefficient) tells us how that variable contributes to explaining the differences among states in terms of economic growth. For many variables, the contribution turns out to be small or nonexistent ("statistically insignificant").

It still might be the case that a given index, while not scientifically constructed, in fact does a reasonable job of including and measuring appropriate variables, excluding inappropriate ones, and weighting them in a sensible fashion. To a significant degree, the legitimacy of an index depends on how well it mimics a more sophisticated statistical approach.

In addition to their lack of statistical underpinnings, there is another reason to question the types of indexes examined here. It is not clear that the concept of business climate or competitiveness for an entire state or metro area makes sense to begin with. Charles Skoro has argued that "the usefulness of the business climate concept depends on the existence of a set of indicators that are *measurable*, that have *substantial effects* on business outcomes, and that are truly *generic*—they influence business activity in a more or less uniform manner regardless of industry, region, or time period" (Skoro 1988). Others have made similar arguments: that the factors important to location and expansion decisions are industry specific, and that the conditions conducive to growth can vary tremendously within a state (and that metropolitan regions, not states, are the focus of business decisions).[1] For manufacturing in particular, the crucial factors may in fact be *project* specific, since access to suppliers and markets will often be key.

So why even bother with an index? Why not just rely on scholarly research to address the policy issues? For example, a recent study by Robert Lynch (2004) reviewed the large body of research on the effects of taxes on growth, and concluded that the effects are small or nonexistent. Most research in this area has found other factors to be more important determinants of business location and investment decisions, namely quality of public services in general and education in particular, utility costs, access to markets, transportation infrastructure, the education level of the labor force, and wage rates. The reason for creating an index, perhaps, is that index numbers, and rankings based on them, are simpler, require little in the way of analytical expertise, and are easier to write about in the popular press.

Five indexes of competitiveness are described and critiqued in some detail in this report. We also review briefly three other rankings or indexes of competitiveness for which there is less information available. Other rankings exist that differ from those reviewed here in that they are explicitly intended to be measures of economic performance or outcomes rather than business climate or competitiveness. Some of these are widely publicized, and we describe these briefly in an appendix to make it clear how they differ from the allegedly causal indexes that are the focus of this report.

In a concluding chapter, we summarize the common themes and methodological problems that characterize the indexes reviewed and present some thoughts on the use and misuse of business climate indexes as a guide to public policy.

CHAPTER 1

The Small Business Survival Index

Since 1996, the Small Business and Entrepreneurship Council (SBEC) in Washington, D.C. has been producing an annual Small Business Survival Index (SBSI), the latest of which was released in October 2004. The report is subtitled, "Ranking the Policy Environment for Entrepreneurship." Unlike most of the other indexes reviewed here, the SBSI does not claim to be an assessment of the overall business climate in a state, but rather a narrower measure of how well a state, through public policies, creates a nurturing environment for entrepreneurial activity and the development of small businesses.

The SBSI is the creation of Raymond Keating, chief economist for the council. The council was recently renamed; it was formerly called the Small Business Survival Committee, a name that is now the title of the "activist and grassroots network" within SBEC, which claims 70,000 members. The council's mission is "to influence legislation and policies that help to create a favorable and productive environment for small businesses and entrepreneurship." It advocates replacing the income tax with either a flat tax, a national sales tax, or a value-added tax, and generally lobbies for lower taxes at the federal and state levels. The council has also published reports critical of government spending, unions, and government regulation.

Are the measures that make up the SBSI appropriate?

While the index purports to be a measure of how well state government supports small businesses and entrepreneurship, the authors apparently believe that there are in fact no government programs or policies that are supportive. The index consists of 23 measures that are described as "government-imposed or government-related costs impacting small businesses and entrepreneurs." The index, in other words, is largely a measure of how heavily a state taxes or regulates business. State spending on infrastructure, the quality of the education system, small business development centers or entrepreneurial programs at public universities, technology transfer or business extension programs, business-university partnerships, small business incubators, state venture capital funding—none of these public activities are considered.

The composition of the index is shown in the list below (with the measures grouped according to our categories, not theirs). For all the tax measures, having lower tax rates (including workers' compensation premiums and unemployment insurance taxes) or no tax at all produces a higher ranking, as does indexing rates and having a tax limitation statute. Being a right-to-work state and having a state minimum wage no higher than the federal improve a state's ranking. Lower health care and electricity costs, a lower crime rate, fewer government employees, "regulatory flexibility," and a "reasonable" liability system are all good things in this index.

Progressive taxes

1. Top personal income tax rate
2. Top capital gains tax rate on individuals
3. Top corporate income tax rate
4. Additional income tax imposed on S-corporations beyond the top personal income tax rate
5. Individual alternative minimum tax ("1" if state imposes AMT, "0" otherwise)
6. Corporate alternative minimum tax ("1" if state imposes AMT, "0" otherwise)
7. Personal income tax rates indexed ("1" if state indexes rates, "0" otherwise)
8. Estate, inheritance, and/or gift taxes (states imposing any of these taxes beyond the federal pick-up tax receive a score of "1," "0" if they do not)
9. Internet access tax ("1" if state has such a tax, "0" otherwise)

Regressive taxes

1. State and local property taxes as a share of personal income
2. State and local sales, gross receipts, and excise taxes (excluding gas tax) as a share of personal income
3. Gas tax (dollars per gallon)

Labor costs

1. Unemployment tax (maximum state tax rate applied to state wage base as a share of state average annual pay)
2. Average workers' compensation premiums (index based on a 2002 study by the Oregon Department of Consumer & Business Services)
3. Right-to-work status ("1" for non-right-to-work state, "0" for right-to-work state)
4. Minimum wage (state minimum minus the federal minimum)
5. Health care cost (ratio of state per capita personal health care spending to the U.S. average)

Government regulations and other

1. Liability system (mean grades based on a survey conducted by the U.S. Chamber of Commerce, where corporations were asked to subjectively assess the fairness and reasonableness of state liability systems)
2. Regulatory flexibility legislation status ("0" for states with "full and active regulatory flexibility statutes" as defined in a study by the Small Business Administration)
3. Tax limitation status ("1" if state has some form of supermajority tax limitation, "0" otherwise)
4. "State and local government bureaucrats" (full-time equivalent employees per 100 residents)
5. Electricity cost (average revenue per kilowatt-hour for electric utilities)
6. Crime rate (crimes per 100 residents)

The rationales offered by the SBEC for including these measures demonstrate the SBSI's single-minded focus on government regulation and taxation as the primary challenges facing entrepreneurship and the growth of small businesses. Modest state estate and inheritance taxes are described as "nothing more than a government hostile takeover at death." The SBSI is concerned that "[h]igh electricity rates due to hefty taxes and heavy-handed, misguided regulations can play a significant part in business decision-making"—as if high electric rates due to weak government regulation of monopoly power are not a problem. High health insurance costs due to "taxes, mandates, and regulations" are a problem, but government efforts to limit the rising cost of medication and medical procedures, and to correct for market failures in the health care sector, are not referenced.

One cannot help but wonder at the inclusion of "government bureaucrats per 100,000 population" in the index. The rationale offered is as follows:

> One rough proxy for regulations can be the number of state and local government employees—or bureaucrats. After all, with regulations, rules, and mandates come regulators, i.e., those dreaming up, writing, passing, monitoring, and enforcing such measures. Obviously, regulators and regulations raise the costs of doing business. A large number of government employees also means that a significant share of individuals are basically performing far less productive work than if they were in the private sector.

It is surprising that kindergarten teachers "regulating" their students, policemen enforcing the traffic laws, and snow plow drivers "monitoring" streets are lumped together as heavy-handed, unproductive bureaucrats hindering the development of the local economy.

It is clear that the selection of index measures was guided largely by the SBEC's ideological stance: anti-government, anti-tax, anti-regulation. The index does not appear to rely on research regarding the effects of public policies on small business formation, innovation, or growth.

Small business growth and survival is not synonymous with entrepreneurial activity, though SBEC appears to treat them so. Many small businesses are not entrepreneurial in the sense of being innovative; much new retail activity, for example, is merely responding to the growth of markets in a cookie-cutter fashion (Goetz and Freshwater 2001). Those who have studied the development of innovation and entrepreneurial activity find that it is generated by some combination of human capital (an educated workforce), financial capital (the availability of venture capital and higher-risk loans), ideas, and a set of intangibles that make up an entrepreneurial culture or climate. One attempt to measure the influence of these factors found that the level of education in the workforce, the level of patent activity and innovation research grants (as a measure of ideas), and the availability of capital together explained 60% of the variation in state entrepreneurial activity (Goetz and Freshwater 2001).

Of the factors contributing to entrepreneurial activity, the public sector has most influence over human capital, which of course requires investment of tax dollars in public education and university research. The variables in the SBSI are largely irrelevant to the development of innovation, and in fact are counterproductive to the extent that they favor smaller government expenditure.

What drives the SBSI?

While there are 23 variables in the SBSI, it turns out that a small number really determine whether a state ranks in the top 10 or the bottom 10. This is because many of the variables do not exhibit much variability, and the SBSI does not re-scale the variables, but simply uses the raw numbers and adds them together. Eight variables range from 0 to 1, and for two others the difference between the maximum and minimum scores is less than 1. The top tax rate variables, on the other hand, range in value from 0 (in states with no income tax) to 9.35 (capital gains rate) or 9.9 (individual income tax) or 9.99 (corporate income tax). The range is even wider if one considers that states with an income tax get an added point if they also have an alternative minimum tax, and another point if their rates are not indexed. When all nine of the measures of progressive taxes are combined, the scores on the combined measure range from 0 (in Nevada and Wyoming, which have no individual or corporate income taxes and no estate or inheritance tax) to 30.94 (California). On the other hand, a combined measure of the level of regressive taxes (property, sales, and excise taxes) ranges from 4.4 to 13.8, and the five indicators of labor costs when combined range from 2.3 to 8.7.

Suppose we divide the 50 states into quintiles based on their overall SBSI: the top 10 states (those with the lowest scores, lower being "better" on this index), the next 10, and so on to the bottom 10 (those with the highest scores). We then compute the average score on each of the four major components of the index for each quintile: the nine mea-

TABLE 1   Average value of the SBSI and of its components, by SBSI quintile

	State quintile					Difference: bottom 10	
	Top 10	Second 10	Middle 10	Fourth 10	Bottom 10	minus top 10	
	Lowest SBSI ◄─			──►	Highest SBSI	Number	% of total
Progressive taxes	7.5	15.7	19.9	23.5	27.8	20.3	89%
Regressive taxes	9.3	8.2	9.4	8.8	10.4	1.1	5%
Labor costs	4.3	4.1	3.7	4.4	5.7	1.4	6%
Other variables	13.5	14.0	12.9	14.1	13.3	-0.2	-1%
Total:							
Overall SBSI	34.5	42.0	45.9	50.8	57.2	22.7	100%

Source: Author's analysis of SBSI.

sures of progressive taxes, three measures of regressive taxes, five indicators of labor costs (health care costs, unemployment insurance rates, workers compensation insurance rates, absence of right-to-work laws, and presence of a state minimum wage above the federal), and the other six miscellaneous variables. **Table 1** displays the results.

Only for progressive taxes is there a consistent and substantial progression from lower to higher values as you move from the top to the bottom quintile. If we look just at what determines whether a state is in the top 10 or the bottom 10, we see that the mean overall SBSI goes from 34.5 to 57.2, a difference of 22.7. Of that 22.7 point difference, 20.3 points, or 89%, consists of the increase in the progressive tax component. The other three components, representing 15 individual measures out of the 23, together account for only 11% of the difference. This is seen more clearly in **Figure A**. The overall SBSI rises from quintile to quintile as the progressive tax component rises; the other components vary little from one quintile to the next.

In the end, then, the Small Business Survival Index is, at best, a crude index of the level of progressive taxes in a state and little more. It is crude because the measures of tax burden themselves are faulty. They do not take into account such important factors as the base to which the tax rate applies or credits allowed. This is particularly crucial in the case of the corporate income tax and its definition of taxable income, rules for apportionment, allowable deductions, and credits for investment, jobs, or research and development. The measures of the personal income tax do not take into account the size of personal exemptions or credits, the

FIGURE A   **Average value of components of the SBSI, by quintile**

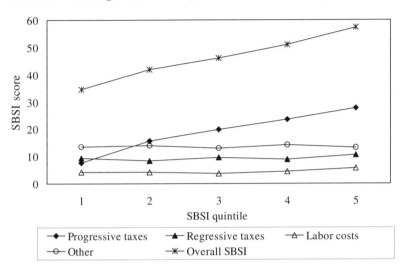

Sources: Author's analysis of SBSI.

size of the standard deduction, or the existence of child care or earned income credits. The SBEC believes, apparently, that the most crucial determinant of the viability of small businesses in a state, and the vitality of the entrepreneurial sector, is income tax rate levels.

How well does the SBSI predict outcomes?

Fortunately, output measures are available to allow a test of the SBSI. One is the Progressive Policy Institute's New Economy Index for 2002, which includes four measures of small business vitality and entrepreneurship: (1) patents issued per 1,000 workers in 1998-2000, (2) business churning (number of start-ups plus number of business failures as a percent of total establishments, 1997-98), (3) gazelle jobs (jobs in rapidly growing firms as a percent of total employment, 2001), and (4) initial public offerings (IPOs; number and size relative to gross state product, or GSP, 2000 and 2001).[2] We also examine data on the formation rate of employer firms (new firms during 2003 as a percent of all firms that had employees at the start of 2003).[3]

**TABLE 2   The SBSI and measures of business vitality:
correlation between the 2001 state SBSI and various outcomes measures**

Measure	Correlation with SBSI
Patents issued, 1998-2000	(0.19)
Patents issued, 1996-97	(0.20)
Initital public offerings, 2000 and 2001	0.11
Initital public offerings, 1997	(0.19)
Job churning, 1997-98	0.36 **
Job churning, 1995-96	0.15
Jobs in gazelle firms, 2001	0.27 **
Jobs in gazelle firms, 1997	0.22
Annual small firm net expansion rate, 1995-2000*	0.04
Employer firm formation rate, 2003	0.30 **

*Firms with fewer than 500 employees; number of firms expanding employment less number contracting employment, as a percent of firms at start of year.
**Significant at the 5% level (one-tailed test, hypothesis that correlation is positive).

Source: Author's analysis of data from the SBSI, the Progressive Policy Institute (2002), and the U.S. Small Business Administration (2004a and 2004b).

Table 2 looks at the correlation between the 2001 SBSI (which does not differ materially in its construction from the 2004 index) and these seven measures of small business vitality in the same or earlier years for the New Economy Index measures or in the 2001-03 period for the Small Business Administration (SBA) data.[4] We use the earlier index on the grounds that the "policy climate" as of a particular year should explain activity in that year or in subsequent years.[5]

The SBSI does not appear to have much relation to the performance of the small business sector and entrepreneurial activity. There is actually a negative correlation with the number of patents and with initial public offerings in 1997; in other words, states with higher SBSIs had fewer patents and IPOs. The other measures in Table 2 are only weakly correlated with the SBSI, if at all; only three are statistically significant. Given the variety of public policies that should be expected to affect small businesses and the likely impact of state economic conditions on business growth, it should not come as a surprise that an index that roughly measures tax burdens on upper-income taxpayers, and not much else, appears to have little to do with small business survival.

TABLE 3   Rank on outcomes measures

	2001 SBSI rank	Patents 1998-2000	IPOs 2000-01	Gazelle Jobs 2001	Firm expansion 1995-2000	Self employ-ment 2000-03	Propri-etor's income 2002-03	Firm formation 2003
Top five								
Nevada	1	24	30	29	13	3	29	1
South Dakota	2	50	34	15	34	35	1	50
Washington	3	9	1	1	18	19	38	3
Wyoming	4	35	34	48	46	48	5	19
Florida	5	22	19	10	23	5	42	4
Bottom five								
Minnesota	46	8	13	16	3	26	20	30
Kansas	47	36	34	22	29	6	4	29
Maine	48	44	22	39	2	47	28	40
Hawaii	49	40	34	50	50	44	37	17
Rhode Island	50	19	34	19	15	1	33	35

Source: Author's analysis of data from the SBSI, the Progressive Policy Institute (2002), and the U.S. Small Business Administration (2004a and 2004b).

Correlations do not signify causality. For example, the small negative correlation between the SBSI and patents issued doesn't prove that lower progressive taxes *hurt* the development of patentable inventions. A rigorous investigation of the predictive power of the SBSI would require a regression analysis that controlled for other factors thought to affect business formation and survival to determine if the SBSI had any independent explanatory power. SBEC does not perform this test.

Another way of looking at the performance of the SBSI is to examine how the best five and the worst five states, according to the SBSI for 2001, ranked on the outcome measures in Table 2. **Table 3** shows the results. The states that supposedly were the best in fact were among the worst on a number of measures. South Dakota (No. 2 in SBSI) and Wyoming (No. 4), in particular, were among the worst-performing states on a number of measures, coming in last or nearly last on some. Similarly, some of the worst five states in terms of the SBSI were among the top states on some measures of business growth and vitality. Minnesota (No. 46) was among the top 20 in five of the seven measures, and Rhode Island (No. 50) was among the top 20 on four, including a No. 1 ranking in the self-employment measure.

A consulting firm evaluating various business climate rankings in Maine concluded that the Small Business Survival Index is "purely an ideological exercise, with no logic behind it" (Lawton and O'Hara 2004). The SBSI purports, at least by its title, to measure how well state government supports and nurtures entrepreneurship and small business development. In fact, it is at best a crude measure of the level of progressive taxes. As such, it leaves out most of the factors that actually have a significant impact on small business survival and entrepreneurship. Creating the index, however, allows the SBEC to argue for lower progressive taxes, and for less government in general, on the grounds that such policies will stimulate small business development and the state economy. A rough attempt to identify a relation between the SBSI and a variety of measures of small business growth and vitality finds little or no relation. In fact, many of the "best" states on the SBSI do poorly compared to their peers on objective measures, and some of the "worst" states, according to SBEC, do well. Whatever the merits of the SBEC economic development philosophy, the SBSI fails dramatically as a guide to state policy toward small business.

CHAPTER 2

The State Business Tax Climate Index

The Tax Foundation published its first State Business Tax Climate Index (SBTCI) in May 2003. Its second annual index was released in October 2004 and incorporated several substantial revisions to its methodology. In fact, the October report contains revised rankings for 2003 based on the new methodology, as well as new rankings for 2004. We will focus here only on the 2004 index.

The Tax Foundation's report is, in some ways, at the opposite end of the spectrum from the Small Business Survival Index. It has an aura of respectability and objectivity and avoids the blatantly ideological arguments for smaller government and lower taxes. Instead it relies heavily on an argument for tax "neutrality," which has the effect of making the analysis itself appear neutral.

The Tax Foundation claims that the index was developed "using the economic tax literature as our guide" (p. 6). In fact, though, it references the literature selectively. A number of recent comprehensive assessments of the vast research on the role of taxes in economic growth have been performed, and their conclusions do not support the argument made by the Tax Foundation that "taxes matter a great deal to business" (p. 15). For example, it quotes an early paper by Michael Wasylenko but ignores his comprehensive review of the research in 1997 that led him to conclude: "Taxes do not appear to have a substantial effect on economic activity among states" (Wasylenko 1997, 47).[6]

What is tax neutrality? A neutral tax is one that does not create incentives for firms or individuals to change their behavior—to invest more or less, to work more or less, to locate in one place rather than another, to employ more or less labor or more or less capital, to use more or less of one kind of capital rather than another, to produce more of one product and less of another, to postpone investment or accelerate it.

The approach of the Tax Foundation in applying this legitimate standard reflects a bias similar to its selective reference to the economic tax literature. "States that do not impose a corporate income tax are clearly achieving a perfectly neutral system in regard to corporate income and so receive a perfect score. States that do impose a corporate income tax generally will score well if they have a flat, low tax rate system. States with complex, multiple-rate systems score poorly."

This argument has a number of flaws. While a zero corporate income tax is in one sense neutral by definition, in a broader sense it is anything but. A state with no corporate income tax must levy other taxes to finance government. It may mean that the state has a higher property tax as a result, which penalizes capital-intensive but low-profit businesses. Nor must a tax system be "low" to be "neutral." A tax system that applies heavy burdens in a way that does not create preferences for different conduct can be quite neutral. The Tax Foundation argument makes it clear what it really thinks is important: low taxes, not neutral taxes.

Nor is its equating of flat rates with simplicity sensible. What really complicates an income tax, among other things, are the multitude of tax preferences—investment and jobs tax credits, R&D tax credits, deductions for investment in an enterprise zone, preferences given to foreign-source income, rules for allocating non-business income, etc. These are not considered anywhere in the index, yet they have a great deal to do with the actual business tax burden. And they are what make a tax decidedly non-neutral.

Another key deficiency in the SBTCI is that it considers only state taxes, despite the fact that local taxes are, on average, comparable in size to state taxes. And there is substantial variation among states in the proportion of taxation that occurs at the state versus the local level. The foundation's approach is heavily biased to give poor ratings to states where the state government collects most of the taxes and provides most of the services, and good ratings to states where the local governments carry more of these responsibilities. For example, Wyoming ranks seventh best on the SBTCI, but Wyoming had the seventh highest *local* tax burden, and instead of being a low-tax state is actually third highest when measured by state and local taxes as a percent of personal income.

What measures make up the SBTCI?

The SBTCI has five main components: the corporate income tax index, the individual income tax index, the sales and gross receipts tax index, the unemployment tax index, and the fiscal balance index. Each of these five components is weighted equally in creating the overall SBTCI, and each is a simple average of two sub-indexes, generally one related to tax rates and the other to the tax base. The sub-indexes, in turn, are constructed from a number of measures. The measures are weighted equally (with a few exceptions) in producing the sub-index. The varying number of sub-index components results, however, in an apparently accidental variation in weights given individual components. Where the measures are continuous variables (e.g., tax rates), they are re-scaled such that the lowest rate is given a value of 10 (the best score) and the highest rate a value of 0 (the worst score). A tax rate that is, say, 80% of the highest rate, would have a score of 2; a rate that is halfway between the highest and lowest rates would have a score of 5, etc. Where the measures are 0-1 variables (1 if the state has a tax feature, 0 if it does not), these 0-1 variables are simply added together, and the resulting totals are re-scaled to assume values from 0 to 10 for the sub-index.

The corporate income tax index

The corporate income tax index is a simple average of two sub-indexes: the tax rate index and the tax base index. The states that rank the best on the combined index are deemed to have a "neutral" corporate income tax, while those that rank the lowest have a corporate income tax that is "poorly designed and represents a serious impediment to business activity."

The corporate tax rate sub-index is composed of four measures:

1. The top marginal tax rate (lower is better)
2. The taxable income level at which the highest rate kicks in (higher is better)
3. The number of tax brackets (fewer is better)
4. The average width of the brackets (narrower is better)

The latter three are intended to measure "the economic drag created by multiple-rate systems." It is unclear why multiple-rate systems are likely to create an "economic drag." The hypothesis that such trivial details as the number of tax brackets has a meaningful economic impact is certainly not supportable. The goal appears to be to skew the sub-index to punish states with progressive rate structures. If the state went from two brackets to one (a flat rate), it would automatically get the top score possible on three of the four measures (2, 3, and 4).

The corporate base sub-index is composed of five measures, each weighted equally:

1. The weight given to sales in the apportionment formula—100% being a perfect score, 33% being the worst—with penalties assessed for adopting the throwback rule and rewards for allowing a firm to choose, from among alternative apportionment formulas, the one that is most advantageous
2. The number of years allowed for carrying net operating losses (NOL) backward and forward (more is better), with penalties for states that cap the amount of NOL carried back or forward
3. The rate of tax on capital stock (no tax is best)
4. The differential between the top corporate and individual income tax rates (the bigger the differential, the worse, regardless of which is higher)
5. A potpourri of other tax base variables: use of federal income as the state base (good); conforming with federal depreciation and depletion (good); presence of an alternative minimum tax (bad); deductibility of foreign, federal, and other state taxes (good); and indexation (good)

It is curious that in some of these categories a better rating is given for provisions that make the tax *less* neutral. For example, the existence of a throwback rule is precisely designed to make the tax system more neutral relative to location decisions. Likewise, single sales factor apportionment (100% sales in item 1) is explicitly designed to favor exporting firms over local-market firms. What these and other policies favored by Tax Foundation have in common is not a connection with the principle of tax neutrality, but that they lower corporate tax levels.

The Tax Foundation was criticized, apparently, for failing to take many important base issues into account in the 2003 index.[7] However, its response was to throw a wide variety of base measures together with no regard to their relative effects on tax burdens. Allowing a corporation to deduct federal taxes from state taxable income, for example, can have a large effect on state tax liability, yet this feature counts as just one-third of one of the six factors that go into the fifth component of the base sub-index. In other words, it counts for 2.5% or less of the overall corporate income tax base sub-index.[8] In contrast, the differential between the corporate and individual top rates, an often meaningless measure, counts for 20%.

The individual income tax index

The individual income tax index is constructed in similar fashion. It includes local income taxes, in the few states where these are allowed, as well as state income taxes. The rate sub-index is made up of two equally weighted factors:

1. The top marginal tax rate
2. The graduated rate structure: the income level at which the top bracket kicks in (higher is better); the number of brackets, with the standard deduction and exemptions considered equivalent to an additional bracket (fewer is better); and the average width of brackets (narrower is better)

All of these features combine to measure the burden on high-income taxpayers—in absolute as well as relative terms. Couching the reduction in number of brackets in terms of tax simplification allows groups to disguise their espousal of reductions in progressivity.

The individual income tax base sub-index consists of four equally weighted factors:

1. The marriage penalty (bad)
2. "Double taxation" of capital income (bad)
3. Differential between the top individual and corporate rates (the smaller the better)
4. Six other issues: use of federal income as the base (good), existence of an alternative minimum tax (bad), existence of a "jock tax" (bad),[9] bracket indexing (good), recognition of limited liability companies and S corporations, and the deductibility of other state taxes, foreign taxes, and federal taxes (good), on "double taxation" grounds

Most of these factors also reflect a preference for lower taxes on higher-income taxpayers. In particular, low or zero taxes on capital income and allowance of the deduction of federal income taxes have an enormous effect in reducing effective tax rates on the very rich (although they hurt neutrality). Federal deductibility in Iowa, for example, reduces the effective top marginal rate from 8.98% to about 5.8%. But once again, these factors are weighted irrationally, the taxation of capital income counting for 25% of the sub-index but the deductibility of federal taxes just 3% or less.[10]

The sales and gross receipts tax index

The sales and gross receipts tax index consists of two equally weighted sub-indexes:

1. Rate: the maximum combined state and local sales tax rate in the state
2. Base: seven equally weighted factors, the first six reflecting the taxation of agricultural inputs; service inputs; manufacturing machinery and equipment, utilities, and raw materials; computer software; leased and rented vehicles or lodging; and pollution control equipment; and the seventh combining the excise tax rates on motor fuels, tobacco, and beer

It is certainly odd to take the highest local sales tax rate to represent the sales tax level for the entire state.

The unemployment insurance tax index

The unemployment insurance index comprises two sub-indexes:

1. Rates: two equally weighted factors, consisting of (1) actual 2003 rates (maximum and minimum, lower being better) and the 2003 taxable wage base (lower is better); and (2) potential 2004 rates (minimum and maximum rates under the most favorable and least favorable tax rate schedules)
2. Base: experience rating formula, charging methods, and other issues

The fiscal balance index

The fiscal balance index, despite its name, does not measure either the balance in the tax system (relying on a mixture of taxes) or the balance between revenues and expenditures (or imbalance, often referred to as a structural deficit). Instead, it is an overall measure of tax levels and constraints on taxation and spending, made up of two equally weighted sub-indexes:

1. State tax collections: average of the state's ranking for FY2003 on state tax collections per capita and on state tax collections as a percent of state personal income
2. Tax and expenditure limitations: percentage vote of the legislature required to pass a tax increase (ranges from 50% in states without a supermajority rule, to 75%), and whether a state has an expenditure limit, a revenue limit, or both (both being best)

The fiscal balance index has no apparent connection to tax neutrality, but instead is simply a measure of current tax levels and the difficulty of raising taxes or spending.

How well does the SBTCI measure business tax burdens?

Since the SBTCI is an attempt to measure only one component of the business climate—taxes—it is most appropriate to evaluate its performance not in terms of its correlation with growth (since the Tax Foundation does not claim that it is the sole determinant of growth) but in terms of how well it compares with other measures of the taxes that fall on business. A recent study by Robert Tannenwald of the Boston Federal Reserve Bank develops what is probably the best measure to date of the maximum state and local tax rate on business.

Tannenwald points out that any attempt to measure taxes falling on business must confront the thorny question of tax incidence—how much of a particular tax is actually paid by business, and how much is shifted to consumers or to workers? The Tannenwald study counts all taxes that are nominally paid by business as taxes falling on business, even payroll taxes that most economists believe are borne at least in part by employees. It represents the *maximum* tax a business could face, if no shifting could occur. Thus the Tannenwald measure is not perfect, but it is far better than the Tax Foundation measure, which of course also counts all taxes nominally paid by business as part of the "tax climate" but fails to measure anything resembling the actual tax paid.

TABLE 4   The SBTCI versus Tannenwald's business tax rate measures: correlations between SBTCI index values and Tannenwald's tax rates

	Tannenwald: business taxes as a percent of:	
	Business profits	Personal income
SBTCI		
Corporate income tax	-0.16	-0.16
Overall index	-0.05	-0.08

Source: Author's analysis of data from the SBTCI and Tannenwald (2004).

Tannenwald constructs two measures of the average business tax rate in a state: total state business taxes collected divided by total business profits earned in the state, and total state business taxes collected divided by total state personal income. The two measures, it turns out, are highly correlated (0.91). In **Table 4**, the Tax Foundation's corporate income tax score and the overall state business tax climate index are compared with Tannenwald's two measures of average business tax rates.

When the SBTCI index values are correlated with Tannenwald's average tax rate measures, the correlations are negative and quite small. (The SBTCI was first converted to its inverse, to produce an index where the highest value represented the highest tax burden, consistent with Tannenwald's measures of tax rates.) For the corporate income tax component of the SBTCI, the negative correlations mean that there was actually a tendency for states with a "better," low-tax score to have *higher* tax rates on Tannenwald's measures. For the overall index, the correlation is almost nonexistent.

This total lack of a meaningful relationship can also be seen by comparing the rankings of the states in terms of the SBTCI versus Tannenwald's tax rates. In **Table 5**, we see that the SBTCI is particularly egregious as an indicator of the lowest tax states. All of the top five states on the overall SBTCI (those with supposedly the lowest taxes) are in the bottom half of the states on Tannenwald's measure (that is, they actually have relatively high tax rates). Alaska, ranked third lowest-tax on the SBTCI, has the highest average tax rates on profits or income.

**TABLE 5   State rankings on the SBTCI versus Tannenwald's average
tax rates**

	Tannenwald ranking (1 = lowest tax rate)			Tannenwald ranking (1 = lowest tax rate)	
	Profits	Income		Profits	Income
SBTCI: **Overall index**			**SBTCI: Corporate** **income tax**		
Top five states			*Top five states*		
South Dakota	32	36	South Dakota	32	36
Florida	37	23	Nevada	27	32
Alaska	50	50	Washington	45	46
Texas	31	38	Wyoming	49	49
New Hampshire	26	30	Colorado	4	8
Bottom five states			*Bottom five states*		
Rhode Island	41	34	Kansas	22	23
West Virginia	47	48	Pennsylvania	11	10
Minnesota	10	16	North Dakota	46	47
New York	36	42	Alaska	50	50
Hawaii	35	28	Michigan	20	12

Source: Author's analysis of data from the SBTCI and Tannenwald (2004).

Minnesota stands out among the highest-tax five on the SBTCI, but it
has the 10th or 16th *lowest* tax rates on Tannenwald's measures.

The picture is essentially the same if we look at the SBTCI corporate income tax component. Of the top five lowest-tax states on the
SBTCI, four are in the *high-tax* half on Tannenwald's tax measures. Of
the bottom five states on the corporate tax index (the five highest-tax
states), three are in the top 25 lowest-tax states (with below average tax
rates) on the Tannenwald measures. Michigan, which has the worst corporate income tax climate according to the Tax Foundation, actually
has the 12th or 20th lowest average tax rate.

For purposes of assessing the competitiveness of a state's tax system in attracting new business or expansions, Tannenwald has argued
that one would ideally measure not the average but the marginal tax rate
—the tax bite on income generated by new investment in a state—a
measure that would take into account the whole array of state and local
tax incentives available for new investment (Tannenwald 1996). **Table 6**
looks at such marginal effective rates for manufacturing firms in 20 states
in 1998, based on research by Peters and Fisher using a representative

TABLE 6   State-local effective marginal tax rates on manufacturing investment, 1998, versus Tax Foundation 20-state rankings for 2003 (1 = lowest or best)

	Peters & Fisher: Effective Corp. Income Tax Rate	Tax Foundation: Corporate Income Tax Index	Peters & Fisher: Effective Overall Business Tax Rate	Tax Foundation: Overall Business Tax Climate Index
Florida	10	2	15	1
Indiana	11	9	20	3
Tennessee	13	10	12	4
Massachusetts	18	13	8	10
Texas	6	7	19	2
Illinois	15	12	5	8
Michigan	7	20	6	15
Pennsylvania	20	19	14	9
Virginia	16	1	11	5
Missouri	9	4	10	6
North Carolina	8	11	7	13
South Carolina	1	3	1	7
Wisconsin	17	8	9	17
Kentucky	5	18	4	18
Connecticut	14	6	13	14
Iowa	2	17	2	12
Minnesota	12	14	16	19
New York	3	5	3	20
Ohio	4	15	17	11
California	19	16	18	16
Correlation:	0.08		-0.34	

Effective marginal tax rate rankings are from Peters and Fisher (2003). The rankings are based on marginal tax rates, calculated as the increment in state and local taxes resulting from new manufacturing investment divided by the increase in before-tax income attributable to the new investment in that state, for multistate manufacturing firms, after taking into account state and local tax incentives. The Tax Foundation rankings are for 2003 using the revised methodology, as published in the 2004 report.

Source: Author's analysis.

firm model of the kind recommended by Tannenwald that takes into account state and local tax incentives for new investment or job creation as well as income, sales, and property taxes. The 20 states are then ranked on this marginal effective tax rate measure and on their SBTCI index numbers for 2003 (using the revised methodology, from the 2004 report). Table 6 compares state rankings in terms of the effective marginal corporate income tax rate from Peters and Fisher versus the corporate income tax component of the Tax Foundation study, and then compares them in terms of the overall marginal business tax rate (Peters and Fisher) versus the overall SBTCI.

The corporate income tax rankings are positively correlated, but the correlation is low. For example, Iowa ranked 17th out of 20 on the Tax Foundation index, making it a high-tax location by the foundation's lights, but was second lowest in taxes on the marginal effective corporate tax rate (due largely to single-factor apportionment and the deductibility of federal taxes, both of which count little in the Foundation index and which more than offset Iowa's high top rate, which counts for a lot in the Foundation's report).

The overall business tax rate or climate rankings are negatively cor-related; the states with higher Foundation rankings (lower taxes) tended to have lower rankings on the overall marginal tax rate (higher taxes). Indiana, third among the 20 states on the overall SBTCI, actually had the highest overall marginal tax rate (it ranked 20th), due in large part to high property taxes, ignored by the Foundation's index. Florida, first on the SBTCI, was 15th in terms of tax rate. New York, on the other hand, ranked at the bottom by the Tax Foundation, had among the lowest overall tax rates on new investment, due largely to generous incentives. Though the rankings are based on tax systems in two time periods separated by five years, the table certainly provides no support, once again, for the contention that the SBTCI is measuring anything relevant to business location decisions.

The Tax Foundation might object to this critique of the SBTCI, ar-guing that the foundation is attempting to measure tax neutrality, not tax levels. But the foundation makes it clear that it believes that a zero tax is the most neutral tax of all. This position allows it to argue for reduced taxes on business in the guise of more economically efficient, "neutral" taxes. That its real objective is lower taxes, not greater efficiency, is clear from its choice of measures, a number of which reward states for imposing taxes that are lower but *less* neutral. Further, the principal justification for the SBTCI is that "taxes matter to business," and the foundation's arguments in support of this assertion are couched in terms of the *level* of business taxes.

There is no point, really, in trying to assess whether the SBTCI suc-cessfully predicts which states will do better in attracting business in-vestment, creating jobs, or the like. If it does, it is purely by accident, for the index does not even measure the effect of a state's tax system on a firm's cost of doing business. Even if the index appeared to be corre-lated with growth, one could not conclude, as the Tax Foundation would like us to, that lower taxes cause growth. The index does not measure tax rates to begin with, or even correlate with relative business tax lev-els. As a tool for assessing public policy, it is fatally flawed, notwith-standing its carefully groomed appearance of plausibility and academic credentials (however spurious).

CHAPTER 3

Beacon Hill's Competitiveness Reports

The Beacon Hill Institute at Suffolk University in Boston first published a "State Competitiveness Report" in 2001. In 2002, the report was expanded to include rankings of the 50 largest metropolitan areas and was renamed the "Metro Area and State Competitiveness Report." The most recent of these annual reports was released in 2004. All of the reports consist of an "index of competitiveness."

What measures make up the Competitiveness Index?

Beacon Hill, in the 2002 report, asserted that it had more variables in its index, 38, than did its competitors. (With the entry of the Pacific Research Institute into the index wars in 2004, however, Beacon Hill can no longer make this claim, as PRI has escalated the number to 219.) In the 2004 report, BHI uses 42 variables for the state index, and 39 for the metro index, to construct eight sub-indexes. The sub-indexes and component variables are listed on the following pages, where "S" denotes a variable appearing only in the state index, "M" a variable only in the metro index, and "+" or "-" indicates whether the variable is assumed to have a positive or negative affect on competitiveness. For example, taxes have a negative sign, indicating that higher taxes produce a lower index value, while budget surpluses have a positive sign, meaning that larger surpluses produce a higher index. (The higher the overall index value, the better, or the more "competitive.") For variables with an asterisk, the measure is for the state in the state index, for the particular metro area in the metro index. (For some variables included in the metro index, the statewide measure is used.)

Government and fiscal policies

State and local taxes as a percent of personal income, 2003 (-)

State workers' compensation premium rates, 2002 (-)

State bond rating (composite of S&P's and Moody's, scale 1-25), 2004 (+)

Bond rating of main cities and counties (M) (+)

Budget surplus as a percent of gross state product, 2003 (S) (+)

Average benefit per first payment for unemployed, 2003 (-)

Full-time equivalent state and local government employees per 100 residents, 2004 (S) (-)

Security

Reported crime per 100,000 inhabitants, 2002 (S) (-) *

Percent change in crime index, 2001-02 (-) *

Murders per 100,000 inhabitants, 2002 (-) *

Thefts per 100,000 inhabitants (M) (-)

Violent crimes per 100,000 inhabitants (M) (-)

Score on the Better Government Association's "Integrity Index,"[11] 2002 (S) (+)

Infrastructure

Percent of households with installed phones, 2004 (S) (+)

High-speed broadband lines per 1,000 residents, statewide, 2003 (+)

Air passengers per capita, 2002 (+) *

Travel time to work, 2003 (-) *

Electricity prices per million BTU, statewide, 2002 (-)

Average rent of two-bedroom apartment, 2004 (-) *

Human resources

Percent of population without health insurance, 2003 (-) *

Percent of population age 25 and over that graduated from high school, 2003 (+) *

Unemployment rate, not seasonally adjusted, 2003 (-) *

Students enrolled in degree-granting institutions per 1,000 residents, statewide, 2003 (+)

Percent of adults in the labor force, 2003 (+) *

Infant mortality rate, deaths per 1,000 live births, statewide, 2001 (-)

Non-federal physicians per 100,000 inhabitants, statewide, 2002 (+)

Percent of fourth grade public school students at or above "proficient" in mathematics, 2003 (S) (+)

Technology

Academic R&D per $1,000 gross state product, statewide, 2001 (+)

National Institutes of Health (NIH) support to institutions, per capita, 2003 (+) *

Patents per 100,000 inhabitants, 2003 (+) *

Science and engineering graduate students per 100,000 inhabitants, statewide, 2001 (+)

Science and engineering degrees awarded per 100,000 inhabitants, 2001 (S) (+)

Scientists and engineers as percent of labor force, 2003 (+) *

Percentage of total wage and salary jobs in high technology industries, 2001 (S) (+)

High-tech payroll as percent of total payroll (M) (+)

Business incubation

Total deposits (commercial banks and savings institutions) per capita, 2003 (+) *

Venture capital investment per capita, statewide, 2002 (+)

Employer firm births per 100,000 inhabitants, statewide, 2003 (+)

IPO (A weighted measure of the value and number of initial public stock offerings of companies as a share of gross state product), 2001 (S) (+)

Percent of labor force that is represented by unions, 2003 (-) *

Minimum wage, 2004 (S) (-)

Entrepreneurial Activity Index (M) (+)

"Cost of Doing Business Index"[12] (M) (-)

New publicly traded companies, statewide (M) (+)

Openness

Exports per capita, statewide, 2003 (+)

Incoming foreign direct investment per capita, 2001 (S) (+)

Percent of population born abroad, 2003 (+) *

Environmental policy

Toxic release inventory, on-site and off-site, total (new and original industries), pounds/1,000 sq. miles, 2002 (-) *

Greenhouse gas emissions (metric tons of carbon equivalent (MTCE) per 1,000 sq. miles), 2000 (S) (-)

Pollution standards index (M) (-)

Serious pollution days per annum (M) (-)

Are the variables appropriate?

Outcome versus causal variables

The most serious problem with BHI's indexes of competitiveness is that they mix causal and outcome variables indiscriminately. BHI claims that its index measures how effectively a state or metro area can compete for economic growth, and its test of the validity of the index is how well the index predicts increases in per capita income. Yet a number of BHI's variables are in fact measures of the *outcomes* or *components* of economic growth, not the causes of it: labor force participation rates, budget surpluses, initial public offerings, entrepreneurial activity, new publicly traded companies, employer firm births. Economic growth tends to draw people into the labor market, increasing labor force participation. It is not clear why one would predict that high labor force participation *causes* growth. Government budget surpluses, likewise, are a *result* of robust income and revenue growth, not a cause. (In fact, a budget surplus can be a drag on economic growth.) And the growth of new firms, small firms, or publicly traded firms is a *component* of overall state or metro area economic growth, not a cause.

Similarly, a number of the variables are simply correlates of high income: the percent of households with phones, the percent with broadband, bank deposits per capita, and the prevalence of high-paid workers (scientists and engineers, high-tech workers). Not surprisingly, where people have more money, they have more money in the bank. And of course states or cities with lots of high-wage workers have higher per capita income.

Other variables are measuring the results of slow growth or low income: the unemployment rate, the percent of households who are uninsured, the infant mortality rate. Surely high infant mortality rates are a result of poverty, not a cause of poverty, and one has surely proven nothing if one shows that states with a high unemployment rate have lower average incomes. Of course they do; losing your job is a sure-fire way to lower your income. And a high unemployment rate is usually the *result* of slow economic growth, or economic decline, not a cause of it.

For other variables in the index, the direction of causality is ambiguous. High bond ratings are partly the result of economic prosperity, which brings with it a growing tax base, ample tax revenues, and low probabilities that governments will default on debt. At the same time, they may be indicative of sound government budgeting practices. Either way, high bond rates may indicate stability of tax rates and spending, which may be appealing to businesses. Low rents might be appealing to someone considering relocation, but they may also reflect a long-term sluggishness in the local economy. Rents, in fact, are sometimes used by economists to measure the overall attractiveness of a locality, since high rents are sustainable only where there is high demand for housing and enough good-paying jobs to support the payments. People want to live there, and can afford to. High rents may be the result of past growth, though they may also at some point become a constraint on future growth.

As Richard Sims has pointed out, the inclusion of variables that measure outcomes, or results of high or low income rather than causes, "...is profoundly circular logic and is equivalent to saying 'we measure things that indicate how well off you are, therefore if you increase these things you will be better off'" (Sims 2003). The mishmash of causal and outcome variables used in the BHI make the meaning of the index incomprehensible.

Dubious variables

Other variables are questionable for other reasons. Air travelers per capita is supposed to be a "sign of a developed infrastructure." But if we look at how the 50 largest cities ranked, it seems that this is a faulty measure. New York City ranked 40th of the 50 cities, while Las Vegas was first and Orlando fourth. Surely what is important to business is the frequency of non-stop flights to important destinations (being a hub for a major airline helps a lot) and lots of competition producing low air fares. New York, with three major airports, should be ranked highly on those factors. Passengers per capita just doesn't capture what is important, and is strongly influenced by high tourist travel in a relatively small metro area. Then there is the indicator "percent of population that is foreign born," included on the grounds that "the more foreigners relative to the native-born population, the more motivated the workforce." This is a dubious supposition.

Missing variables

Another problem with BHI's index is that many of the variables are missing for many of the states or metro areas. For all but two of the 42 state variables, data were missing for 10 to 14 of the 50 states; for one variable they were missing for 17 states, and for one they were missing only for two. Among the states, the number of missing variables ranged from four in Washington to 18 in North Carolina. Thus the overall index, and the six sub-indexes or eight components, are measuring different things for different states. This factor alone renders it of doubtful value.

The situation for the metro area index is just as bad. The average city score is based on data for only 31 of the 39 measures; 21% are missing. The number of missing data items per city ranged from four to 14 (36% of the total). Consider the openness sub-index, consisting of two measures: percent of population that is foreign born, and exports per capita for the state. In five cities, openness is based only on the percent foreign born; in eight cities it is based only on exports; in four cities it is based on neither; and in the remaining 33 it is based on both. (Curiously, in the four states where there are data for neither measure of "openness," the city nonetheless receives a score, the basis for which is not explained.)[13] Or consider the infrastructure index, which contains five variables. For Tampa, Fla. and Portland, Ore., it is determined only by electricity prices and the number of broadband lines per 1,000 residents, while in Phoenix it is determined by rent, travel time, and air passengers. It is difficult to put any credence in comparative index values when they are measuring one set of things for one city, a different set for another.

What's left?
Of the 42 variables in the state model, how many are at least plausible measures either of (1) a component of the cost of doing business in the state, (2) a measure of amenities or other factors that could be important in attracting labor, or (3) a correlate of labor productivity? These would constitute the first pass at a list of the variables that are logical to include in an index of competitiveness. To better understand the index, what drives it, and how well it predicts, we have reorganized the variables into eight categories, including the above three. The number of measures in each category is indicated for states and cities:

Potential business costs (6 state measures/5 city measures)
State and local taxes as a percent of personal income
State workers' compensation premium rates
Average benefit per first payment for unemployed

Electricity prices per million BTU, statewide

Percent of labor force that is represented by unions

Minimum wage (S)

Labor productivity (education) (3/2)

Percent of population age 25 and over that graduated from high school

Percent of students enrolled in degree-granting institutions per 1,000 residents, statewide

Percent of students at or above "proficient" in mathematics, grade 4, public schools (S)

Amenities (7/9)

Reported crime per 100,000 inhabitants (S)

Thefts per 100,000 inhabitants (M)

Violent crimes per 100,000 inhabitants (M)

Percent change in crime index, 2001-02

Murders per 100,000 inhabitants

Travel time to work

Non-federal physicians per 100,000 inhabitants, statewide

Toxic release inventory, on-site and off-site, total pounds/1,000 sq. miles

Greenhouse gas emissions (metric tons of carbon equivalent (MTCE) per 1,000 sq. miles) (S)

Pollution standards index (M)

Serious pollution days per annum (M)

Technology capacity (7/6)

Academic R&D per $1,000 GSP

NIH support to institutions in the state, per capita

Patents per 100,000 inhabitants

Science and engineering graduate students per 100,000 inhabitants, statewide

Science and engineering degrees awarded per 100,000 inhabitants (S)

Scientists and engineers as percent of labor force

Percent of total wage and salary jobs in high-technology industries (S)

High-tech payroll as percent of total payroll (M)

Components of growth (5/6)

Venture capital investment per capita, statewide

Employer firm births per 100,000 inhabitants, statewide
IPOs as a share of gross state product (S)
Exports per capita, statewide
Incoming foreign direct investment per capita (S)
Entrepreneurial Activity Index (M)
Cost of Doing Business Index (M)
New publicly traded companies, statewide (M)

Outcomes of growth (4/3)
Bond rating (composite of S&P's and Moody's, scale 1-25)
Budget surplus as a percent of gross state product (S)
Unemployment rate, not seasonally adjusted
Percent of adults in the labor force

Income correlates (5/4)
Percent of households with installed phones (S)
High-speed broadband lines per 1,000 residents, statewide
Percent of population without health insurance
Infant mortality rate, deaths per 1,000 live births, statewide
Total deposits (commercial banks and savings institutions) per capita

Other (5/4)
Full-time equivalent state and local government employees per 100
    residents
Air passengers per capita
The BGA Integrity Index (S)
Average rent of two-bedroom apartment
Percent of population born abroad

The variables in the last four categories simply do not belong in a causal index of competitiveness. The 16 in the first three categories are at least plausible components, though of course which of them are in fact significant causal factors is an empirical question that is best addressed through statistical analysis. As for the six or seven in the "technology capacity" category, they are factors that at least plausibly increase the likelihood that a state will experience growth in high-tech sectors of the economy.

Scaling and weighting

Every measure in the BHI indexes carries an identical weight of 1 within its sub-index. This weighting scheme is described by BHI as "democratic," a term one is not likely to encounter in the typical statistics text, statisticians generally preferring criteria such as "valid," "reliable," or "consistent." Each measure is also normalized so that it has a mean value of 5.0 and a standard deviation of 1.0. The BHI sub-indexes, then, are simple averages of the component-normalized variables. Each sub-index is normalized in the same fashion, and the overall index is a simple average of the six sub-indexes. This normalization creates the same degree of variability for each variable, and then for each sub-index. Combined with the equal weighting, this guarantees that each measure within a sub-index contributes in the same proportion to the overall sub-index, and each sub-index contributes identically to the variation in the overall index.

Is this even-handedness a virtue? It does prevent a situation such as we found with the SBSI, where the tax variables exhibited large variation while others varied little from one state to another. The result was that the state rankings were driven almost entirely by the handful of tax measures that exhibited most of the state-to-state variation, a result that was not acknowledged by the authors or apparent to the user. With BHI's index, at least we know that each variable indeed counts the same. But this is a virtue only if it is true that each variable *should* contribute equally. As with the choice of weights, the decision to normalize is entirely arbitrary unless there is a valid reason to force equality of contribution. Such decisions should be made on the basis of actual knowledge of the relative importance of the variables in producing growth, or some other outcome.

In the case of the BHI index, the normalization and weighting produce some effects that are counterintuitive, to say the least. For example, the percent of the population that is foreign born has a doubtful connection to economic growth, yet it is twice as important in determining the overall state BHI score as the state's average price of electricity, unambiguously a real business cost. This is because the foreign-born measure is one-third of the "openness" sub-index, while electricity prices count for just one-sixth of the "infrastructure" sub-index, and these two sub-indexes are weighted equally in the overall index. As a result, the fact that electric rates are twice as high in Illinois as in Idaho is more than offset by the fact that 12.3% of the Illinois population is foreign born, compared to only 4.8% in Idaho.[14] (Remember: the foreign born are supposed to be more "motivated" than domestic workers.) Considering just these two measures, BHI in effect concludes that Illinois has a much better business climate. For metro areas, the disparity is even more pronounced, with the percent foreign born constituting 50% of the "openness" component, while electricity prices are just 20% of the "infrastructure" sub-index.

Does BHI's index work?

To its credit, BHI puts its index to the test, and reports the results of a regression analysis that attempts to predict differences in real per capita income across states at a point in time on the basis of the BHI competitiveness index and real per capita income the previous year. BHI finds that the two variables together explain 35% of the state-to-state variation in per capita income (in statistical terms, it reports an R^2 of 0.35). It also finds that an increase of one point on the overall index (which would be a quite sizeable increase, the index ranging from 2.9 to 7.3) is associated with $877 higher per capita income (it reports a coefficient of 877 on the index, statistically significant at the 5% level). BHI found a coefficient of 0.5 on the previous year's per capita income (also statistically significant), indicating that about half the per capita income differences in 2002 carried over to 2003.

The BHI results are suspect, however, because of the state cost-of-living index used to convert state per capita income to real per capita income. BHI relied on the ACCRA price index for metro areas for 2002 and 2004, a price index that changed dramatically and inexplicably between those years for some states, and which the producers point out should not be used to compare changes in the cost of living over time.[15]

To test the BHI results we performed three analyses:

- BHI's analysis was recalculated using a better measure of interstate cost-of-living differences, one that relies on fair market rent data from the U.S. Department of Housing and Urban Development to adjust the official CPI-U (consumer price index for all urban consumers) for interstate differences in median housing and utility costs. In this analysis, the BHI index was not close to being statistically significant, even at the 10% level.[16]

- A test to determine whether the BHI index predicts which states experience more *growth* in per capita income (comparing 1999 and 2004) produced a similar result: the BHI index was not significant.[17]

- As a further test, we attempted to explain differences in state real per capita income in 2003, adjusted using the state cost-of-living index based on fair market rents, on the basis of the first seven components identified above (business costs, education, amenities, technology capacity, growth correlates, growth outcomes, and income correlates.) The last component, "other," was omitted because its odd collection of variables doesn't seem to belong anywhere else. Not surprisingly, the only variable that was a statistically significant predictor of differences in real income was the last, the set of variables that are correlates of income.

On the basis of its one, dubious regression analysis, BHI concludes: "Competitiveness really does matter" (BHI 2004, 10). In fact, it claims that the "index and its sub-indexes are powerful tools policymakers can use to improve their areas' affluence" (BHI 2004, 10). Take Tennessee, for example, which ranks a poor 41st on the overall index. What can policy makers do to increase the state's competitiveness and hence the well-being of Tennesseans? They should work on areas where they are most deficient, such as "security" and "technology." BHI then claims that, if Tennessee could raise its scores on these two sub-indexes to the national average, "it could raise its overall index to 4.81 and in the process raise its real per capita personal income by almost $600."

Let us suppose that, somehow, the BHI index does indeed predict, to a degree, which states experience more growth in per capita income over some time period. It is an enormous leap of faith to then assert that any given state can embark on public policies to, say, lower taxes or increase the percent of households with high-speed Internet, and that such a state should then expect its per capita income to grow in conformance with the regression. One simply cannot infer anything about particular policies from the aggregation of policies and outcomes that is the BHI index. It could well be that all of the index's predictive power is due to the set of variables that are in fact outcomes or components of growth, or correlates of higher income, and that the real "policy" variables have nothing to do with income growth, and changing them would have no impact.

Since BHI's overall Competitiveness Index is an odd collection of potential causal variables, outcomes variables, components of growth, correlates of income, and other unjustified measures, it is of no use as a guide to public policy.

CHAPTER 4

The Cato Institute's
Fiscal Policy Report Card

The Cato Institute, a libertarian think tank in Washington, D.C., released its seventh biennial *Fiscal Policy Report Card on America's
Governors* in March 2005; this was the report card for 2004. One might
surmise from the title that this is an assessment of how well America's
governors manage state finances—balancing budgets, maintaining revenue and expenditure stability over the business cycle, ensuring tax fairness and budget transparency, etc. In fact, Cato claims that it is "the
only objective analysis of the fiscal performance of the nation's governors" (Cato Institute 2005, 14). The "grades" are based, however, only
on "an index of fiscal restraint" for each state. Put simply: "Governors
who cut taxes and spending the most receive the highest grades" (p. 2).
And the reason Cato gives for focusing on tax and spending cuts is that
"states that reduce taxes improve their prospects for economic growth"
(p. 12). This series of reports, in other words, represents another attempt to rank states based on one dimension that is merely presumed to
rank competitiveness: tax and spending policy.

The 2004 Fiscal Policy Report Card produces an overall grade—A,
B, C, D, or F—for each of 42 governors (six having been in office for
too short a period to be graded, and two excluded for technical reasons).
The governors also receive separate grades for spending restraint and
for tax policy. Behind each letter grade is a "score," which is an index
summarizing several spending, revenue, or tax rate variables.

Most of the measures making up Cato's scores represent changes
during the governor's tenure in office, so that the time period will vary
from state to state. Five of the variables measure actual changes in spend-

ing or revenue, reflecting legislation passed and signed. Another five variables represent simply the governor's position, or the change that would have occurred if the governor's tax or budget recommendations had been followed. Five of the tax rate variables are a combination: they represent the actual change plus any change recommended by the governor but not enacted. This focus on the governor's leadership and policy proposals makes the Cato index unique among those reported on here.

What measures make up the Fiscal Report Card?

Cato's overall fiscal policy score is based on 15 variables, organized in three categories. Where the time period ends in fiscal 2002, the measure applies only to governors in office before that year. With one exception (noted below), each measure receives equal weighting in the overall score. The tax rate measures with an asterisk in the list below are those where the change in rates is the sum of the actual and governor's recommended changes. A plus sign indicates that a higher value for that variable is associated with a higher grade; a negative sign indicates that a higher value is associated with a lower grade.

Spending (4 variables)
Average annual percent change in real per capita direct general spending, actual, through fiscal 2002 (-)
Average annual percent change in real per capita general fund spending, according to governor's recommendation, through fiscal 2005 (-)
Average annual percent change in direct general spending per $1,000 of personal income, actual, through fiscal 2002 (-)
Average annual percent change in general fund spending per $1,000 of personal income, according to governor's recommendation, fiscal 2002 – fiscal 2005 (-)

Revenue (5 variables)
Average annual percent change in real per capita tax revenue, through fiscal 2002[18] (-)
Average annual percent change in tax revenue per $1,000 of personal income, through fiscal 2002[19] (-)
Average annual recommended change in general fund revenue per $1,000 of personal income, through fiscal 2005 (-)

Average annual percent change in real per capita general fund revenue, fiscal 2002 – fiscal 2005 (-)

Average annual percentage tax cuts or increases recommended by the governor, through fiscal 2005 (+)

Tax rates (6 variables)

Percentage point change in the top personal income tax rate * (-)

Percentage point change in top corporate income tax rate * (-)

Sum of top marginal personal and corporate income tax rates in 2004 (weighted one-half) (-)

Change in sales tax rate * (-)

Change in gasoline tax rate * (-)

Change in cigarette tax rate * (-)

Before an overall score is computed, each of the variables is converted to an index number, where the state with the "worst" performance (highest rate of growth in revenue or spending) receives a zero and the "best" performing state is assigned a value of 100. This normalization process creates a similar degree of variability (defined here as the range rather than the standard deviation, as in the BHI normalization procedure) across the measures to prevent some measures from dominating the overall score differences. The four expenditure variables are averaged to produce a spending restraint score, and the remaining 11 variables are averaged to yield the tax score. All 15 are averaged for the overall score.

What drives the Fiscal Report Card?

The overall score is determined by actual and recommended changes in tax rates, revenue, spending, and growth, with these factors receiving the following weight in the score:

Tax rate cuts	(38%)
Revenue reductions	(34%)
Spending cuts	(28%)

Clearly, the report card is little more than a measure of how aggressively governors push the Cato Institute's agenda of limited government by cutting spending and taxes; there is not much pretense that it is about anything else. Still, the index shows that not all tax cuts are created equal. Cutting income taxes by increasing personal exemptions or increasing the standard deduction, or by enacting a state EITC or enlarging a child care credit, are OK in that they reduce tax revenues, but they are clearly inferior policies, in Cato's view, to cutting the top rates. A cut in the top rate produces a larger score improvement compared to an increase in the standard deduction that produces an equal revenue loss, because the rate cut shows up in two tax rate measures in addition to the revenue measures.

More importantly, the index reveals the indiscriminate nature of an agenda focused exclusively on "limited government." Whatever the level of government spending in a state, whatever the quality of public services, there is too much government. All spending cuts are equally good, whether they cut a wasteful economic development subsidy or child health care. All spending increases are equally bad, whether to subsidize an indoor rain forest in Iowa or to raise teacher's salaries up from the bottom in Alabama. Tax expenditures, corporate tax loopholes favoring out-of-state corporations, and sales tax exemptions for special interests are all good policies, because they reduce revenue. Efficiency, effectiveness, and fairness are not factors in evaluating a governor's fiscal performance.

How does the Fiscal Report Card perform?

The Cato Institute does not subject its index to a test directly. Instead, it cites selected research that supports Cato's argument that fiscal stringency produces economic growth. This procedure gives Cato license to sprinkle the report with statements such as: "Some governors are heeding the warning that states cannot tax their way back into prosperity" (Cato Institute 2005, 11).

The Cato Institute, apparently, disagrees with Nobel Prize–winning economist Joseph Stiglitz, who has argued persuasively that increasing spending and increasing taxes during a recession will actually benefit a state's economy more than a policy of cutting spending and cutting taxes (Orszag and Stiglitz 2001). This outcome can result because spending cuts produce direct unemployment and loss of income to public workers, as well as reduced purchases from suppliers to state government, while much of a tax cut leaks out of the state's economy through out-of-state purchases and additional savings. With the opposite policy—spending and tax increases—the economic logic works in a state's favor: the direct employment and purchasing effects from more spending outweigh the loss of in-state consumer spending from the tax increase.

The Cato report includes a table that purports to show that tax-cutting states experienced more growth than tax-hiking states during the period 1990 to 2002. The authors make it impossible to replicate or verify their results, because they do not tell us the identities of the 10 tax-hiking and 10 tax-cutting states, nor when taxes were cut or increased, nor how they defined a tax cut or an increase, nor the magnitude of such changes.[20]

It is likely that Table 4 in the Fiscal Report Card study was created in similar fashion to an analysis by the same author (Stephen Moore, senior fellow at the Cato Institute) published one month after the 2002 report card: "States Can't Tax Their Way Back to Prosperity: Lessons Learned From the 1990-91 Recession."[21] In that report, the top 10 tax cutters and tax hikers are identified in two tables: one listing the states that cut or increased the top personal income tax rate the most, the other listing the states that cut or increased the top corporate income tax rate the most. In these tables, Moore includes among the supposed tax cutters states that cut rates only in the last few years of the decade. In fact, five of the 10 "corporate tax cutters" did not cut tax rates until 1997 or later. North Carolina actually *raised* the top corporate rate in 1991, but Moore attributes all of the above-average growth in North Carolina from 1990 to 2001 to the tax cuts phased in between 1997 and 2000. In fact, North Carolina grew more *prior* to 1997 (and after the tax *increase*) than it did *after* 1997 and the tax cuts. Similarly, Vermont and New Hampshire actually decreased their tax rates between 1987 and 1996, yet Moore puts them in the "tax hiker" category and attributes their slow growth between 1990 and 2001 entirely to the fact that they increased their top corporate income tax rates in 1997 and 1999, respectively. Furthermore, it may well be that the states that grew the most in the first part of the 1990s were in the best position to cut taxes in the latter 1990s—in other words, causality runs in the opposite direction. The late tax cuts may have been caused *by* the early growth. Yet the Moore analysis, by ignoring the timing, concludes that the late tax cuts were the cause *of* the growth. This is bogus research, plain and simple.

To put the Cato report's argument to a simple test, we performed a regression analysis using the Cato scores from the 2002 Fiscal Report

Card on the five variables representing actual spending and revenue changes through fiscal 2000 to predict percent changes in per capita income across states from 2000 to 2003. In other words, we created a single score or variable for the regression analysis that was comparable to Cato's overall score, but excluded all the component variables that incorporated merely recommended changes, as opposed to actual changes.[22] We used the 2002 rather than the 2004 data in order to allow estimation of the effects of these variables on subsequent growth rates; the five variables in the 2002 report are identical (except for time period) to those used in the 2004 report. Finally, we included per capita income at the start of the period, 2000, as a second explanatory variable. There were 36 states in the analysis (six of Cato's 42 states had no data for the spending and revenue variables). Note that the magnitude of changes is incorporated, and the tax and spending changes occurred prior to the start of the growth that we are trying to explain, so that causality (if any) cannot run in the opposite direction.

The per capita income variable was significant and negative (higher income states at the start of the period experiencing slower *growth* in income subsequently, and vice versa). The coefficient on the Cato score was not close to statistical significance even at the 10% level. Similar results were found with models predicting growth from 2000 to 2003 and from 1999 to 2003, with the tax rate variable entered separately and the composite score based only on the four spending/revenue variables. Neither the tax rate nor the composite score were near statistical significance for either time period. In other words, there was no discernible tendency for states that scored well on Cato's measures of spending and revenue restraint in the latter 1990s, or on Cato's measures of top income tax rates, to experience more rapid income growth during the subsequent recession.

To provide a further test, we also looked at an earlier period: state policies during the recessionary period of the early 1990s versus subsequent state growth during the boom period of the latter 1990s. We used data from the 1996 Fiscal Policy Report Card to construct a composite score based on actual spending and revenue changes through fiscal 1994 and an index based on the top corporate and individual income tax rates. These became explanatory variables in a regression model (along with per capita income in 1994) predicting growth in real per capita income from 1994 through 1998. The results were similar: Cato's measures of fiscal restraint and low tax rates did not help explain which states grew more rapidly.[23]

In the 2004 Report Card, Cato spends considerable time arguing that the fiscal problems of states in the 2001-04 recession years "resulted from out-of-control spending" during the 1990s. They also claim that "the states that had the top 10 highest rates of growth in revenue per $1,000 in personal income between 1995 and 2002 had larger deficits as a percentage of state spending than the 10 states that had the lowest revenue growth rates" (Cato Institute 2005, 10). How much lower? Was the difference statistically significant? We are left to guess. No numbers are presented, and the identities of the 20 states are not revealed. Why the top 10 and the bottom 10? Why not look at all 50 states?

A recent report by Robert Zahradnik, using research methods that are clearly explained and results that are transparently presented, finds quite the opposite. Looking at all 50 states, he found that states began cutting taxes in the mid-1990s, and that the bulk of the tax cuts were enacted in the 16 states that cut taxes by at least 7%. In those 16 states, he found: "fiscal year 2004 budget deficits averaged 14.9% of spending. This compares to budget deficits of 'only' 8.9% of spending for the other 34 states" (Zahradnik 2005, 1). He also found that the top 16 tax-cutting states cut spending the most between 2002 and 2004 and raised taxes the most. Tax cutting worsened the fiscal crisis.

Zahradnik's report also addressed the issue of tax cutting and economic growth. He found that the 16 states that cut taxes the most between 1994 and 2001 lost 1.5% of total payroll employment between 2001 and 2003, compared to just 0.5% job losses in the states that cut taxes less. The 16 most-tax-cutting states also had lower growth in personal income (4.4% versus 5.8%) and a greater increase in the unemployment rate (1.4 percentage points versus 1.0). The differences are even larger if one compares the six states that cut taxes more than 10% between 1994 and 2001 with the other 44 states. The six states lost 2.3% of payroll employment, versus 0.6% for the other 44.

While Cato's Fiscal Report Card may provide some summary indication of how states and governors performed relative to one another in terms of increasing or decreasing tax rates, revenues, and spending, there is no evidence that this tells us anything about state economic performance. The policy conclusions that Cato would like to draw from this report are simply not supported.

CHAPTER 5

The Economic Freedom Index

The newest entrant into the index wars is the Pacific Research Institute (PRI), which in 2004 released its first U.S. Economic Freedom Index. The PRI's index, however, was an update of a 1999 index, Economic Freedom in America's 50 States, produced by researchers at Clemson University and published by the State Policy Network. The genealogy is traced further back to a pair of reports issued periodically since the mid-1990s that compare nations: the Index of Economic Freedom (the Heritage Foundation and the *Wall Street Journal*) and the Economic Freedom of the World index (published by the Cato Institute and the Fraser Institute).

According to the PRI report: "Economic Freedom is the right of individuals to pursue their interests through voluntary exchange of private property under a rule of law. This freedom forms the foundation of market economies" (PRI 2004, 12). The index is purported to measure "how friendly (or unfriendly) each state government is toward free enterprise and consumer choice." Why should policy makers be concerned about "economic freedom?" Because when states limit such freedom "people flee economically oppressive states and residents are made poorer" (PRI 2004, 6).

What makes up the Economic Freedom Index?

The EFI is the most complex and least transparent of the indexes reviewed. It is not possible to replicate PRI's index numbers with the information provided in its 177-page book, even when supplemented with the "software database" that can be downloaded from PRI's Web site for $50. (Most of the book consists of two-page descriptions of each state's economy.) While the database lists most, but not all, of the raw data with which PRI begins its analysis, and the book shows the final scores on each of five "sectors" and the overall score by state, there is insufficient explanation to reproduce all the steps PRI took to get from the raw data to the index numbers.[24] Nonetheless, there is much we can say about PRI's method.

The overall EFI comprises "scores" or index numbers in each of five "sectors": fiscal, regulatory, judicial, government size, and welfare spending. Unlike the other indexes, the raw variables are immediately converted to rankings, with a rank of 1 given to the state that is "most free" in terms of a variable, and a 50 to the "least free" state. Thus, cardinal data are converted to ordinal data. Many of the variables are 0-1 or yes-no variables, such as the existence of a state prevailing wage or a continuing education requirement for nurses. In that case, a state without the regulation or requirement receives a rank of 1, a state with that regulation a rank of 50. The "score" a state receives for a given sector is a simple average of the state's rankings on each of the variables in that sector.

While starting with 219 variables, PRI eventually reduces them to the 47 that appear in the final score calculations. This was done both by cutting some redundant variables and by combining similar variables into a single one by averaging the state's rank on each of the related variables.[25]

For each of the five sectors, we describe below the overall logic espoused by PRI and a general description of the indicators that make up that sector score. After each of the indicators, we note whether it is an average of the ranks for two or more underlying variables (avg) and/or a binary variable (Y/N).

The fiscal sector

Taxes represent "a government infringement on free markets," according to PRI. Even when taxes "correct inefficient prices" they "distort markets by changing the relative prices of goods and services." This will come as a surprise to economists, who have spent a great deal of effort developing the theory of market failure, which lays out the conditions under which markets fail to produce efficient outcomes and how government intervention to correct distorted prices improves economic efficiency. But in the world of PRI, there is no such thing as a good tax or, apparently, an inefficient unregulated market; the only thing that can render a market inefficient is government. This would also have come as a surprise to Adam Smith, whom they quote favorably, but selectively, for it was Adam Smith who warned: "People of the same trade seldom meet together, even for merriment and diversion, but the conversation ends in a conspiracy against the public, or in some contrivance to raise prices." Monopoly, market power, predatory pricing, collusion, price fixing, false advertising, insider trading—all these habits of unregulated capitalism are absent in PRI's free world.

The tax measures are a mixture of rates and revenues. Since revenues are equal to the rate times the base, a high amount of revenue per capita can reflect high rates (in which case it is double counting with the rate measure) or a strong tax base (in which case the index penalizes states for economic success).

1. Individual income tax: revenue per capita, highest and lowest rates, 2003 (avg)
2. Sales tax: rate and per capita revenue, 2002, 2000 (avg)
3. Excise taxes: gas, diesel, cigarette, and liquor tax rates; per capita tobacco and alcohol tax revenue, 2002-03 (avg)
4. License taxes: total, motor vehicle, corporate, hunting and fishing, and occupation license tax revenue per capita, 2002 (avg)
5. Corporate taxes: lowest and highest corporate income taxes, per capita corporate income tax revenue, 2003 (avg)
6. Debt: per capita revenue minus expenditure, outstanding debt per capita, 2000 (avg)
7. Sales tax exemptions for fertilizer, seed, feed, insecticides, pesticides, groceries, restaurant meals,[26] and custom software (avg)
8. Per capita property taxes, 2000
9. Per capita inheritance, estate, and gift tax revenue, 2002
10. Per capita severance tax revenue, 2002
11. Per capita state tax revenue, 2002
12. Tax freedom day: day average individual stops working to pay taxes, 2003
13. Tax burden on a high-income family, 2001

Regulatory sector

The PRI includes among the regulations that restrict economic freedom state laws requiring public education. They also include minimum wage laws because they infringe "on the right to contract." On the other hand, they applaud right-to-work regulations, which in fact prevent unions from making dues payments or check-offs the subject of collective bargaining. It seems that some rights to freely negotiate contracts are to be protected, others to be outlawed. States that require professionals to obtain licenses in order to practice, or mandate continuing education requirements in certain occupations, receive a score of 50 (very unfree). The market is supposed to take care of such things as professional competence; patients will stop going to an anesthesiologist whose patients die at an inordinate rate, and cities will stop hiring engineers whose bridges fall down. Gun control laws, compulsory workers' compensation and insurance laws, and even minimum ages to obtain a driver's license, restrict desirable economic freedom in PRI's reasoning.

Regulatory measures include:

1. Licensing requirements for 15 non-health professions, 2000 (Y/N) (avg)
2. Licensing requirements for 42 health professions, 2000 (Y/N) (avg)
3. Continuing education requirements for 15 professions, 1999 (Y/N) (avg)
4. Percent of land owned by the federal government, 2000
5. State purchasing requirements giving preference to recycled goods or small businesses, or restricting purchase of environmentally harmful products, and whether or not state purchases recycled products, alternative fuels, or environmentally friendly products, 1997 (all bad) (average of 13 Y/N variables)
6. Labor legislation: minimum wage or prevailing wage laws (bad), right-to-work laws (good), compulsory workers' compensation (bad), workers compensation waivers permitted (good), state insurance mandates on employers, workers' compensation premiums (avg) (all but the last are Y/N)
7. Public school regulation: public school choice and charter school legislation (good) (Y/N), and percent of children in private schools (more is better) (avg)
8. Seat belt laws (Y/N) (avg)

9. Environmental health legislation: laws regulating such things as mercury, lead, and asbestos (average of eight Y/N variables).
10. Minimum driver's license ages (average of two age variables)
11. State public utilities commission full-time-equivalent (FTE) employees (fewer are better), 2002
12. Insurance regulatory agency FTE employees (fewer are better), 2001
13. Index of strictness of gun control laws (from H. Henderson, *Gun Control*, Facts on File)
14. Property rights legislation (according to the organization, Defenders of Property Rights)
15. Corporate constituency statutes (not explained)

The judicial sector

The PRI report confesses that "difficulties arise when including judicial indicators" in an index of economic freedom. In fact, these difficulties lead to several logical contradictions. PRI views positively regulations mandating liability insurance for physicians (because this assures that injured parties are paid) and caps on damage awards (because this helps prevent "excessive awards"). They thus judge states with these regulations as "freer," despite the obvious fact that they are regulations and interfere in free markets. They assume states with tort reform are freer, and states with fewer lawyers are freer. Higher salaries for judges are better because that attracts more experienced, "higher quality" judges. (Higher salaries, of course, require higher taxes, which are bad.) And this logic is not extended to any other public sector activity; it is apparently not important that other public employees be adequately compensated.

The judicial measures include:

1. Number of attorneys (fewer are better), 2003
2. Attorney general's salary (higher is better), 2002
3. Compensation of judges (higher is better), 2002 (avg)
4. Terms of judges (shorter is better), 2001 (avg)
5. Selection of judges (elected = 1, appointed = 50), 2002 (avg)
6. Tort reform, as of 2003 (average of 10 kinds of tort reform, each Y/N)
7. Medical liability reform (mandatory liability insurance, caps on damages—both good), 2003 (avg) (Y/N)
8. Illinois brick repealer statutes (unexplained) (Y/N)

Government size

The PRI analysis assumes that "every state has instituted more government than is required to provide a minimal state to enforce the rule of
law." Therefore, any reduction from the present size represents an increase in economic freedom. Government size measures include:

1. State and local expenditure as a percent of GSP, 1999 (lower is
   better)
2. Government representation: total number of government units (not
   per capita), 2002, and legislators per million population (probably
   more is worse for both measures, but this is not clear), 2003 (avg)
3. Government employment: state and local FTE employees per 10,000
   population (lower is better), and ratio of local FTE government
   employees to total state and local FTE government employees (higher
   is better), 2001 (avg)

The welfare-spending sector

PRI singles out welfare spending as the only component of state budgets (other than the judiciary) worthy of its own sector. It says it is not
concerned about the purpose or merit of welfare programs, by which
it means any transfer program (including food stamps, Medicare, and
Social Security). Instead, PRI is concerned that "they are financed by
an involuntary transfer of private assets; therefore, they reduce economic freedom." The less we spend on lunches for schoolchildren, the
more freedom we have to spend money on what we personally prefer
to purchase. Of course, from the perspective of the hard-pressed ben-
eficiaries and other supporters of the programs, the new "freedom"
from Medicare, Medicaid, and food stamps offered by PRI might not
be well-received. For all of the variables listed below, more or higher
is worse.

1. State and local welfare spending per capita, 2000
2. Medicaid spending per capita, 2000
3. Percent of population receiving public aid, 2000
4. Medicare benefit payment per enrollee, 2001
5. Monthly Temporary Assistance for Needy Families (TANF) benefit
   for a family of three, 2001
6. Average monthly food stamp benefit per recipient, 2002

7. Average monthly benefit per Women, Infants, and Children (WIC) nutrition program participant, 2002
8. Commodity costs for the national school lunch program per recipient, 2002

How well does the Economic Freedom Index predict?

In the Economic Freedom Index, the sector scores are simple averages of the ranks (or scores created by averaging ranks) of the variables making up that sector, so that each of the variables is weighted equally. For example, Nevada's overall regulatory score is influenced equally by its high percentage of federally owned land (83%, giving it a rank of 50), its almost total lack of state purchasing requirements aimed at improving the environment (giving it near the top score of 1), and its merely average rank (29) on the number of FTE employees of the state public utilities commission.

In creating the overall index from the five sector scores, however, PRI goes to great lengths to consider alternative weighting schemes. In fact, it used five different datasets (including the first, with all 219 indicators), by eliminating and combining variables in different ways. Then it experimented with different weights for the five sectors. As PRI describes this process:

> The judgment involved in this process is subjective, but the purpose is to weight sectors and construct indexes in many different ways since there is no absolutely correct method. Sector scores are calculated using each of the five data sets, and weighted using various subjective and objective techniques. (PRI 2004, 40)

In all, PRI ended up with 48 different indexes and settled on Index40, which used dataset 3 (the one outlined above). Why? Because it had "the greatest statistical link to net population migration rates." The weights used in this index were produced by principal components analysis:

0.349 times fiscal score
0.342 times regulatory score
-0.126 times judicial score
0.063 times government score
0.373 times welfare-spending score

In other words, the overall Economic Freedom Index is determined largely by the scores on three of the five sectors, in this order: welfare spending, fiscal, and regulatory. Curiously, the judicial score actually enters negatively; the more "free" a state on the judicial index the less "free" the state is overall. As PRI concedes, this means basically that the measures comprising the judicial score did not work as they expected.

A proper statistical analysis would begin with a model of the migration process, including identification of the major factors known to influence migration rates, such as job opportunities, climate, recreational and cultural amenities, environmental quality, public services (particularly quality of public schools), and the cost of living (particularly housing prices). The economic freedom index would then be included in such a model to see if it has independent explanatory power, when controlling for these other factors. Such a model would be sure to specify that certain variables—those involving government revenue and expenditure, and housing prices—be defined for a period *preceding* the migration to be explained, since causality can run in the other direction (substantial in-migration driving up housing prices, revenues, and expenditures).

What PRI has done is typical of attempts to demonstrate the predictive power, and hence validity, of an index: it conducted a simple one-variable regression model that fails to control for other factors influencing migration. Then it used an index based largely on 2001-03 data to predict migration rates from 1995 to 2000.[27] (This after describing in some detail how the index values and rankings for a number of states changed dramatically from the 1999 index created at Clemson to the 2004 index by PRI. Apparently people migrating in the late 1990s were amazingly prescient.) Worst of all, PRI did not begin with the theoretically most defensible index, test it, and live with the results. Instead, it experimented with 48 different indexes and then picked the one that did the best job of producing the answer it was looking for.

In Chapter 4 of the 2004 report, PRI turns to another test of usefulness: the ability of the Economic Freedom Index to predict differences among the states in per capita income. Here PRI does in fact construct a multiple-regression model with the following explanatory variables: proportion of the population with at least a high school education in 2000, average temperature, population density in 2000, per capita income in 1990, median age in 2000, church membership rate (which it describes as a proxy for the work ethic) in 1990, and the 2004 economic freedom index. These variables are meant to explain differences in state per capita income in 2000. Again, it is not clear why a state's 2004 index, based largely on 2001-03 variables, should explain 2000 income. Also, the model fails to incorporate any measure of the condition of the state's economy, such as the unemployment rate, which would certainly be expected to affect per capita income. Furthermore, the largest component of the Economic Freedom Index is state welfare spending. It is likely that low state per capita income in 2000 meant that the state had to spend more per capita on transfer payments to low-income households; to suggest that high spending on transfers in 2000-02 *caused* low per capita income in 2000 is peculiar. Yet that is the inference that PRI would have us draw from its regression analysis that shows a strong relation between welfare spending (and hence the index) and per capita income.

PRI then goes on to calculate an "oppression tax" for each state. This is the percent reduction in per capita income suffered by the state's residents as a result of their state failing to be No. 1 in economic freedom. In other words, PRI took the results of the regression model, plugged in the value of each of the variables for a given state, but then substituted the value of the Economic Freedom Index for Kansas (the "most free" state). It then compared the per capita income predicted by the model with the state's actual per capita income. The difference is the oppression tax levied on the state's residents for failing to be as up-to-date, freedom-wise, as Kansas. The residents of Rhode Island fare the worst: their tax is 13%; if they simply cut WIC benefits, quit requiring nurses and accountants to have licenses or further their education, lowered income tax rates on the rich, lowered the price of a fishing license, exempted pesticides from the sales tax, got the federal government to cede them all federal land, quit buying recycled oil, started buying more foam cups and plates, fired half the staff of the public utilities commission, lowered the minimum age for a drivers license, got rid of half their attorneys, paid their judges more, sent more children to private schools, provided easier access to hand guns, and a few other things, the state's per capita income would rise $3,600.

CHAPTER 6

Other competitiveness rankings

In this chapter, we review three additional rankings that attempt to identify a city or state's economic competitiveness or business climate. Like those reviewed in earlier chapters, these rankings are multi-dimensional, with the overall ranking based on a composite score or index. Unlike the others, the methodology behind the rankings is viewed as proprietary. The magazine articles or Web sites that present the rankings describe the methodology only in summary terms, if at all, and the variables underlying the index are often not identified. Usually, only the final index score is reported. As a result, we cannot critique these indexes in depth. The three rankings discussed here are:[28]

- Economy.com's "North American Business Cost Review" for states and metro areas

- *Forbes* magazine's "Best Places" ranking of metro areas

- *Expansion Management* magazine's six "quotients" for states, cities, or school districts

Economy.com's Cost of Doing Business indexes

Economy.com (formerly Regional Financial Associates) of West Chester, Pa, has published its annual Cost of Doing Business indexes for states and metro areas since 1994. The indexes are part of a publication titled the *North American Business Cost Review*, the 2003 edition (released in November 2003) being the latest available (for sale) on its Web site as of March 2005. This report presents cost of doing business indexes for all U.S. states and metropolitan areas, as well as Canadian provinces and metro areas.

The State Cost of Doing Business index comprises three sub-indexes: labor costs, energy costs, and state and local taxes. The U.S. Metropolitan Area Relative Business Cost index is similar to the state index, but adds a fourth component: an index of office rents. In both cases, the U.S. average cost for each category is given a value of 100, with each state's cost expressed as a ratio (so that a state with costs 10% above the average has a cost index of 110, for example). Each index is a rolling three-year average of costs, and the overall index is a weighted average of the three sub-indexes.

The components and the actual weights assigned are as follows:

1. Unit labor costs (75% in state index, 65% in metro): wage and salary compensation per dollar of output
2. Energy cost index (15%): average commercial and industrial electric costs
3. Tax index (10%): total state and local taxes, unemployment and worker's compensation premiums, and user charges, as a percent of area personal income
4. Office rents index (10%, metro only): average rent per square foot for Class A office space

The Cost of Doing Business indexes are notable in that they weight the components in a non-arbitrary way, at least according to economy.com: "These weights are assigned based upon the importance of each cost component in explaining long-term regional employment growth." Staff at economy.com explained that the weights "are the result of staff members' research and development of the index itself," but would not elaborate.[29] We are left to wonder if they are actually derived from a statistical analysis of the importance of each component in explaining growth, from a review of the research in this area, or by some other method involving more judgment than empirical measurement.

The unit labor cost measure is calculated for each industry (three-digit NAICS code) in each state or metro area.[30] Sectors producing for local markets (retail trade, construction, real estate, government, services) are excluded from the calculation on the grounds that the business location decisions of concern are based on wages and productivity in export sectors of the economy. The overall labor cost is a weighted average of the sector costs, where the weights are each sector's share of national employment. Thus the weights are the same for every state and metro area, so that overall labor costs are not affected by the mix of industries present. This procedure seems quite defensible.

The energy cost index is a weighted average of the average commercial electricity cost and the average industrial electricity cost, where the weights are the relative importance of commercial and industrial costs at the national level.

The tax index includes all state and local taxes, and most user charges as well, regardless of who ultimately pays those taxes. The vast majority of property taxes are paid on residential and commercial property, and much commercial property is anything but "footloose"—it is tied to location. This is true of residential rental property and retail space, as well as local-market-oriented office activity. Most user charges are paid by households; most economists would argue that taxes on labor (unemployment insurance and workers' compensation premiums) are ultimately borne at least in part by labor, not by business; general sales taxes are largely borne by consumers; and individual income taxes are borne largely by employees. While it could be argued that economy.com's measure overstates business taxes for all states, it would surely not do so in equal proportion; some states rely more heavily on taxes falling directly on business. It is noteworthy that in its other measures economy.com takes pains to focus only on the impacts likely to be felt by mobile economic activity: commercial and industrial electric rates, labor productivity *excluding* local-market activities.

One justification given for including personal taxes is that they affect after-tax wages. This puts economy.com in the position of arguing that firms must fully compensate employees for cost-of-living differences in the form of taxes, but not in the form of utility costs (or housing or anything else, for that matter), and that the greater range and quality of public services associated with higher taxes is for some reason completely irrelevant. This is an indefensible position. The other justification given is that the tax burden on top management and owners is a major determinant of business location decisions. There is no research cited to support this claim, and the same argument applies to management: surely managers care about the quality of the local education system and of public services generally, and these things are associated with higher taxes. It can also be shown that the cost to the firm of paying top management higher salaries to compensate for higher state and local taxes would be a trivial percent of the average firm's total cost of business, an amount swamped by other cost differences influencing location decisions (Ditsler and Fisher 2003).

Although there are problems with the tax component, it is only 10% of the overall index, and the remaining components seem defensible. However, measures of infrastructure quality, transportation costs, and access to markets are absent, and we cannot tell if the weights applied to the three components (or four, in the case of metro areas) are appropriate.

Forbes' Best Places

Since 1999, *Forbes* magazine has published an annual "Best Places" ranking of the 150 largest metro areas and (since 2000) a companion "Best Small Places" ranking (in 2004, consisting of 168 metro areas of 57,000 to 335,000 population). The rankings are intended to show the best places "for business and careers," and thus mix business location considerations with factors presumably influencing labor migration. The overall ranking is apparently based on each city's rank on nine dimensions:

1. Cost of doing business: ranking on economy.com's Cost of Doing Business index
2. Educational attainment: the share of the population over age 25 with at least a bachelor's degree
3. Advanced degrees: Persons with a Ph.D. per 100,000 population
4. Cost of living: an index based on housing costs, utility costs, transportation, and other expenditures
5. Crime rate: overall crimes per 100,000 residents
6. Culture and leisure: an index based on the prevalence of museums, theaters, golf courses, sports teams, and other cultural and recreational facilities
7. Income growth: average annual growth over past five years
8. Job growth: average annual growth over past five years
9. Net migration: average annual rate over past five years

The cost-of-doing-business ranking is based on the North American Business Cost Review produced by economy.com (see discussion at start of chapter). The cost-of-living index is also produced by economy.com. The culture and leisure index is from Sperling's BestPlaces; the Sperling Web site provides no information on this index, however. The remaining variables come from readily available census and economic data. Metro areas are ranked on each of the nine factors; the rankings on each factor are available for each metro area on the *Forbes* Web site. The nine measures are weighted and combined to produce the overall ranking; the cost of doing business and educational attainment are weighted most heavily.[31]

The *Forbes* rankings are based on many of the factors economists generally consider important in business location decisions: operating costs, labor skill and productivity, and factors important in attracting a workforce (cost of living, safety, amenities). Factors missing from the list include health insurance costs, transportation costs and access to national markets and suppliers, and the quality of public services (especially infrastructure and public education). The index does have a bias in favor of skilled labor and white-collar employment, emphasizing as it does the prevalence of a college education among the labor force (two of the nine measures). Interestingly, three of the nine rankings deal with quality-of-life and cost-of-living issues, while the tax bite on business, which figures so prominently in most of the other indexes we review, is just 10% of the cost-of-doing-business index (see earlier).

While the three growth measures appear to be outcomes measures, one could argue that they belong on this list because job seekers naturally look for growing rather than stagnant places. This illustrates the problems involved in creating a single ranking of the best places for business and the best places to start a career. Rapid growth and rising wages, for example, probably signify good places for employees to seek jobs, but businesses may be more attracted by labor surplus areas. Which is the "best place" depends on who you are.

Expansion Management's Quotients

One of the more interesting sets of rankings are the "quotients" produced annually by *Expansion Management* magazine. Each of the six quotients is independent, and they are produced over the course of a year and published in the magazine and online.

1. Health care cost quotient (third annual, February 2005): ranking of the 50 states
2. High-value labor quotient (second annual, March 2004): rankings of the top 50 metropolitan areas
3. Quality-of-life quotient (sixth annual, May 2004): metro areas identified either as "5 star communities" or "4 star communities"
4. Logistics quotient (fourth annual, September 2004): 331 metro areas ranked on 10 dimensions, with the top 50 (rated five stars) and the second 50 (rated four stars) listed
5. Education quotient (14th annual, December 2004): ratings of 2,800 secondary school districts
6. Legislative quotient (10th annual report in December 2004): ranking of the 50 states

All of the six quotients are constructed on the basis of rankings on several dimensions, though the source and even the nature of the data behind these rankings are often not identified, nor is it explained how the overall ranking is derived from the components. The magazine stamps "proprietary information" on all the lists of rankings. The components of the quotients are as follows.

Health care cost quotient
The overall rank is based on rankings in five areas, each based on various measures, only some of which are identified:

1. Health care facilities: hospital beds per 100,000 population, number of "top-notch" health care facilities (from *US News and World Report*'s "Best Hospitals," and Solucient's "Top 100 Hospitals")
2. Health care providers: physicians and nurses per 100,000 population
3. Health insurance costs: average employer payment for single coverage and average employee contribution for single coverage (from the Agency for Healthcare Research and Quality of the U.S. Department of Health and Human Services)
4. Health care provider visit costs: average cost of a visit to a doctor, a dentist, and an optometrist (from the ACCRA cost-of-living index for metro areas)
5. Malpractice costs: Average medical malpractice premiums per doctor (Insurance Information Institute), and the American Medical Association's Medical Liability Crisis rating.

Expansion Management also figured in the state's ranking on Morgan Quitno's *Healthiest State Award,* though it is not specified how this was incorporated. Measures included in the 2004 ranking but not mentioned in the description of the 2005 quotient are the projected nurse shortage, public health workers relative to population, number of teaching hospitals, the poverty rate, the number of community health centers in underserved communities, and the percent of health insurance plans that are highly rated (from the *Consumers' Guide to Health Plans*). It is possible that some of these measures were deleted because in 2004 it was simply the "health quotient," but now has been recast as the "health care cost quotient." It is also possible that some of these measures are in fact part of the 2005 quotient.

High-value labor quotient
1. Percent of population age 25 and older with a bachelor's degree
2. Percent of population age 25 and older with a master's degree
3. Percent of population age 25 and older with a professional degree
4. Percent of population age 25 and older with a doctoral degree
5. Science and engineering workers as a percent of the workforce
6. Patents issued
7. Ranking based on number of community colleges and four-year colleges, and number of colleges and universities offering advanced degrees

Quality-of-life quotient
The quality-of-life quotient is composed of a large number of measures, some of which are left unspecified. Those identified can be grouped as follows:

1. Cost of living: housing affordability index, HUD fair market rents, cost of living, state and local tax burden
2. Income: median family income, per capita income, per capita disposable income
3. Labor market: unemployment rate, average annual pay, average wage, number of workers age 18 to 34
4. Crime: violent crime and property crime statistics from the FBI
5. Transportation: traffic congestion and traffic safety measures based on Federal Highway Administration data, air accessibility from the Federal Aviation Administration

6. Education: the education quotient (weighted average for school districts in the metro area); continuing education opportunities from the *Places Rated Almanac,* number of colleges and universities, percent of population over age 24 with a high school diploma, percent of population over age 24 with a college degree (separately for advanced degrees and for science and engineering degrees)

Logistics quotient

The logistics quotient is constructed in cooperation with *Logistics Today* magazine. The description of the measures underlying the 10 components is quite dubious.

1. Overall transportation and warehousing industry climate
2. Workforce: transportation and warehousing labor costs, size of the workforce, and skills
3. Road infrastructure and spending
4. Road density, congestion, and truck safety
5. Road and bridge conditions
6. Interstate highway access: number of interstates and auxiliary highways
7. Fuel taxes and fees
8. Railroad access: number of freight and Class I railroads serving the area, miles of track, tons of cargo carried, rail safety records
9. Waterborne commerce: number of ocean, lake, and river ports
10. Air cargo service: major carrier service, passenger and freight volume, number of cargo airports

Education quotient

There are three sub-indexes, with the first (graduate outcomes) weighted most heavily in the overall quotient. The sub-indexes were the same in 2003 and 2004, and in the 2003 report components of the sub-indexes were identified.

1. Graduate outcome: average ACT or SAT scores and the graduation rate
2. Resource index: per pupil spending, student-teacher ratio, beginning and average teacher salaries, and possibly other measures

3. Community index: percent of adult population with at least a high
    school degree, percent of adult population with at least a college
    degree, average household income, and the child poverty rate

Legislative quotient

The overall quotient or ranking is based on the state's ranking in each of
seven categories. The measures that go into the rankings in each of these
categories are poorly explained, though from the 2003 and 2004 reports
it is possible to infer that they include at least the measures listed below.

1. General tax bite: tax revenue per capita
2. Five-year trend on spending and taxes
3. Infrastructure spending: share of state budget
4. Education spending: share of state budget
5. "Spending on itself": cost per capita of running the state legislature
6. Debt management: per capita debt, percent of budget spent servicing
    existing debt, and reduction in debt service over past five years
7. Right to work laws (yes or no).

Since each index is in a different format, and some are for states,
some for metro areas, and one is for school districts, there is no attempt
to combine them into an overall index for states or metro areas. Nonetheless, it is of interest what this magazine thinks is important for location executives to consider. As the magazine describes itself:

> The mission of *Expansion Management* is to help educate our readers,
> most of whom run companies with fewer than 500 employees, about
> how best to evaluate and compare various communities and sites
> throughout the country and around the world in order to determine
> which will best satisfy and enhance their long-term business
> requirements. [Our circulation profile consists of] 45,000 executive
> decision-makers—52.7% of whom are in the CEO, Chairman, Owner,
> President category—of companies (with 50-500 employees) that are
> actively looking for the best location to establish a future
> manufacturing plant, distribution center, regional or corporate
> headquarters, call center, or other such business facility.

Contrary to the approach taken by the more ideologically driven indexes described in the preceding chapters, the editors of such a magazine believe that health care, school quality, quality of life, the quality of the state's infrastructure, and labor productivity are all important considerations for their readership when planning a facility expansion or relocation. These features receive equal billing, in fact, with an index relating to taxes, spending, and debt.

The individual quotients by and large seem defensible and are not cluttered with variables that are on the face of it irrelevant or just plain peculiar. Having said that, the high-value labor quotient is largely a measure of the proportion of the population that is highly educated; employers may well have additional considerations in mind when thinking of high-value labor. The quality-of-life quotient seems skewed in favor of upper-middle-class communities, incorporating as it does several measures of income and several measures of the share of the population with college or advanced degrees (though this may well be the bias of corporate location decision makers as well). And it contains no information on factors that other quality-of-life rankings include, such as cultural and recreational opportunities, the quality of public services, and climate. The validity of the health care cost quotient cannot be judged without extensive research into each of its components, and the same can be said of the logistics quotient, about which we can determine little.

The legislative quotient assumes that lower taxes are better and appears to measure this quite simplistically, by overall tax revenue (whether state only, or state and local, is not mentioned), not taxes falling on business. Were it not for the right-to-work indicator, it would be better described simply as the government spending and revenue quotient. It also assumes that the only spending areas of significant concern to business are education and infrastructure.

What can we learn from these indexes?

Two of the three rankings reviewed in this chapter are produced by business-oriented magazines appealing to site location consultants and corporate site location managers. This market gives the rankings a decidedly different flavor from the indexes produced by think tanks with pronounced ideological positions that are trying to influence public policy. The remaining ranking was produced by a private consulting firm.

There are four other rankings of cities or metro areas that differ from those reviewed in this chapter in that they are explicitly intended to be measures of economic performance or outcomes rather than business climate or competitiveness. Some of these are widely publicized, and we describe these briefly in an appendix to make it clear how they differ from the allegedly causal indexes that are the focus of this report. Interestingly, one of these rankings of cities is produced by *Inc.* magazine, which in the early 1980s produced a state small business climate ranking that was fairly broad, incorporating measures of capital availability (25%), labor costs (20%), state support of small business (25%), business activity (20%), and taxes (10%) (Skoro 1988). *Inc.* abandoned its attempts to measure business climate in 1986 and instead began to rank states (and now cities) only according to their performance.

In comparing these three rankings with the five reviewed earlier, a striking difference stands out: these indexes are for the most part based on a much broader set of factors that are defensible as significant determinants of business investment or state growth. In addition, there are far fewer instances of extraneous variables with little theoretical or empirical justification. Still, by viewing the methodology as proprietary, these indexes preclude any independent verification that they in fact are composed of what they claim, and in fact prevent the reader even from identifying all of the factors that make up the rankings. The academic standard of replicability of results cannot be applied. While the creators of the rankings would argue that the lack of transparency prevents others from stealing their product, the privileged nature of the data also protects the products from criticism.

CHAPTER 7

Conclusion: Do business climate rankings serve a useful purpose?

Taking the five state business climate rankings at face value would lead to the following conclusions:

- Massachusetts is the most competitive state (BHI), but is a poor place for small businesses to survive, ranking 41st (SBSI).

- Mississippi is the least competitive state (BHI), but ranks as the seventh best place for small businesses (SBSI).

- Minnesota is the fourth most competitive state (BHI), yet is 48th in terms of business tax climate (SBTCI) and 47th for small business survival (SBSI).

- Hawaii has the worst tax climate for business (SBTCI) but also the 18th *best* tax climate for business (Cato).

- Kansas has the most "economic freedom" (PRI) but is not a very good place for small business, ranking 31st (SBSI).

- New York is among the best in terms of fiscal policy (fourth on Cato's index) but ranks 49th on business tax climate (SBTCI).

Thirty-four of the 50 states can brag that they are in the top 10 in terms of business climate or competitiveness; they just have to pick which of the five indexes they want to point to. Forty-four states are in the top 20 on at least one of the five. Only two states are among the top 15 on all five rankings; no state is in the bottom 15 on all five measures. The average state's best ranking is 26 positions above its worst.

Perhaps more importantly, business interests in just about any state can find at least one ranking to support an argument for cutting business taxes to make the state more competitive. In all but eight states, one can find at least one index that puts the state in the bottom half of all states. Corporations in Minnesota can use the Tax Foundation's 48th-place ranking on business tax climate or the 47th-place ranking on the Small Business Survival Index to push for business tax cuts, despite the fact that, on one of Tannenwald's measures, only nine states have tax rates on business lower than Minnesota's, and Beacon Hill ranks the state fourth best in competitiveness. Business lobbyists continue to push for tax cuts in Iowa despite the state's low business taxes (especially on exporting firms), and in doing so they can appeal to Iowa's poor performance on the SBSI (43rd) and on Cato's Fiscal Report Card (46th).

One might argue that disparities between the indexes is to be expected because they are attempting to measure different things. The overall business climate is not the same as a nurturing environment for small business, nor is "economic freedom" the same as the business tax climate. Yet all of the organizations creating these indexes assert that they are measuring something of critical importance to a state's economic future and its potential for growth. On that basis, they should produce roughly consistent results.

The underlying problem with the five indexes, of course, is twofold: none of them actually do a very good job of measuring what it is they claim to measure, and they do not, for the most part, set out to measure the right things to begin with. The Small Business Survival Index is in fact almost entirely about tax burdens on upper-income residents rather than about state programs or policies to assist entrepreneurship or small business growth. The Economic Freedom Index is a sometimes bizarre collection of policies and laws libertarians love, or love to hate, but few have any plausible connection to a state's economic potential. The State Business Tax Climate Index is a large and complex undertaking but ends up generating a number that has little relation to the actual taxes falling on new business investment in a state. The Beacon Hill Competitiveness Index is a hopeless mishmash of causal and performance variables that render it useless as an overall predictor of anything. And the Cato Institute's Fiscal Policy Report Card is little more than a rating of governors on their aggressiveness in promoting an agenda of limited government.

It is clear that the real audience for all five of these indexes is state policy makers. Some of the reports are broadcast widely to state legislators through the ideological ALEC, the American Legislative Exchange Council. None of the organizations are bashful about drawing conclusions for public officials; they argue, in so many words: "Our index is a guide to what you need to change in state policy in order for your state to prosper." And the factors that make up the indexes clearly are designed to promote a particular political agenda: in most cases, the agenda is limited government, low taxes, spending cuts, and less regulation.

Do the businesses making investment and location decisions pay any attention to these state rankings? Here it is instructive to look at the publications aimed at corporate location executives and site location consultants. As we saw in Chapter 6, such publications do indeed like to publish rankings of places. A striking difference, however, is that the business magazine rankings are much broader in scope. The two that are aimed at creating an index of growth potential or competitiveness look at the whole range of factors that are important to business and/or to employees, including labor costs, cultural and recreational amenities, climate, energy costs, transportation, educational attainment, school quality, and health care. Tax levels are part of the equation, but only a small part. Most of the other, and more important, factors are either not amenable to change through legislation, or can be improved only through active government programs, which tends to mean increased spending and taxation. That is no doubt why we don't find them among the criteria of the limited government, anti-tax think tanks.

It is precisely because the competitiveness indexes produced by the ideological think tanks are aimed at promoting particular kinds of legislation that they do a poor job of predicting state economic growth: the measures used must pass an ideology screen, so the validity and relevance criteria go by the wayside. This is also why the indexes are probably ignored by the business people actually making the decisions.[32] They should be ignored by policy makers for the same reason.

APPENDIX A The overall state rankings

	Small Business Survival Index		State Business Tax Climate Index		Competitiveness Index (BHI)		Cato's Fiscal Policy Report Card		Economic Freedom Index	
	Score	Rank	Score	Rank	Score	Rank	Score	Rank	Score	Rank
Alabama	39.4	8	5.66	16	3.68	46	48	27	25.9	25
Alaska	43.8	20	6.85	3	5.01	27			27.8	33
Arizona	42.8	17	5.49	19	4.60	32	49	25	21.9	11
Arkansas	45.0	24	4.44	43	3.69	45	52	18	25.1	23
California	59.9	50	4.61	38	5.14	22	42	39	38.8	49
Colorado	39.9	9	6.35	8	6.27	5	76	1	18.8	2
Connecticut	50.1	34	4.70	37	5.57	15	58	9	35.2	48
Delaware	44.5	23	5.57	18	5.43	18	54	14	20.9	8
Florida	34.3	5	6.93	2	4.81	29	67	2	25.1	22
Georgia	44.4	22	5.44	20	5.08	24	64	3	24.1	19
Hawaii	59.6	49	3.74	50	3.67	47	52	18	28.0	35
Idaho	45.6	25	4.85	31	5.58	14	53	15	19.0	4
Illinois	43.6	19	5.21	23	4.22	39	49	25	32.8	46
Indiana	39.9	10	5.74	12	4.12	42	52	18	22.7	14
Iowa	55.1	43	5.03	28	5.57	15	46	33	23.4	16
Kansas	48.6	31	4.82	32	6.05	10	48	27	18.2	1
Kentucky	47.5	29	4.35	44	4.31	38	53	15	29.1	39
Louisiana	49.9	32	5.06	27	3.16	49	44	37	29.2	40
Maine	57.5	46	4.44	42	4.36	36	47	32	26.9	30
Maryland	44.0	21	5.42	21	5.29	19	46	33	26.5	27
Massachusetts	53.2	41	4.80	33	7.29	1	56	13	29.4	41
Michigan	36.9	6	4.70	36	5.08	24	58	9	27.9	34
Minnesota	58.8	47	4.06	48	6.45	4	48	27	31.1	44
Mississippi	37.8	7	5.15	25	2.93	50	53	15	26.5	27
Missouri	43.2	18	5.84	11	5.21	20			21.8	10
Montana	52.2	38	5.63	17	4.92	28	58	9	24.6	21
Nebraska	50.2	35	4.77	35	6.22	6	52	18	24.2	20

(cont.)

APPENDIX A *(cont.)* **The overall state rankings**

	Small Business Survival Index		State Business Tax Climate Index		Competitiveness Index (BHI)		Cato's Fiscal Policy Report Card		Economic Freedom Index	
	Score	Rank	Score	Rank	Score	Rank	Score	Rank	Score	Rank
Nevada	26.9	2	6.49	6	4.33	37	63	4	22.1	12
New Hampshire	41.4	14	6.63	5	6.11	7	48	27	20.2	7
New Jersey	56.6	44	4.78	34	3.84	44			30.2	42
New Mexico	50.5	36	4.50	40	4.50	33	60	6	28.4	37
New York	57.5	45	4.04	49	4.43	34	63	4	39.5	50
North Carolina	51.2	37	4.86	30	5.06	26			25.6	24
North Dakota	46.7	26	4.50	39	5.86	11			24.0	18
Ohio	53.2	40	4.87	29	3.92	43	45	36	30.9	43
Oklahoma	47.9	30	5.68	14	4.42	35	40	40	19.6	6
Oregon	52.7	39	6.15	10	5.57	15	58	9	26.9	29
Pennsylvania	40.5	12	5.31	22	4.79	30	30	42	31.6	45
Rhode Island	59.1	48	4.25	46	4.72	31			33.2	47
South Carolina	41.0	13	5.18	24	4.15	40	50	23	22.4	13
South Dakota	24.6	1	7.37	1	5.13	23	50	23	23.3	15
Tennessee	41.7	16	5.67	15	4.13	41	60	6	26.2	26
Texas	40.0	11	6.80	4	5.21	20	40	40	23.5	17
Utah	46.9	28	5.10	26	6.94	2	48	27	19.4	5
Vermont	54.7	42	4.31	45	6.10	8	46	33	28.0	36
Virginia	41.5	15	5.74	12	6.08	9			18.9	3
Washington	33.9	4	6.25	9	6.81	3	60	6	27.3	31
West Virginia	50.0	33	4.24	47	3.58	48	44	37	27.7	32
Wisconsin	46.8	27	4.46	41	5.66	13			28.8	38
Wyoming	31.5	3	6.45	7	5.69	12	52	18	21.2	9

Note: For some indexes a higher score is better, and for other indexes a lower score is better. In all cases in the above table a ranking of 1 is "best" and 50 is "worst."

Source: Author's analysis of indexes.

APPENDIX B   The 50 largest metropolitan areas ranked

City/metropolitan area by population size	Ranking among the 50 largest metropolitan areas for each index			
	Forbes: Best Places	Economy.com: Cost of Doing Business	*Expansion Management*: High Value Labor Quotient	BHI: Metro Area Competitive-ness
Los Angeles	47	48	24	32
New York	41	51	16	35
Chicago	38	32	17	37
Boston	19	50	1	3
Washington, DC	3	31	2	
Philadelphia	24	38	14	33
Houston	5	14	20	24
Atlanta	4	11	18	10
Detroit	49	36		31
Dallas	11	8	22	12
Riverside	34	46		
Phoenix	9	23		21
Minneapolis-St Paul	7	27	13	5
Orange County	18	44	15	
San Diego	6	49	8	13
Nassau-Suffolk	17	35		
St Louis	44	19		30
Baltimore	30	25	9	
Tampa	42	24		28
Seattle	46	34	9	1
Oakland	26	47	4	
Miami	50	28		23
Pittsburgh	21	30		29
Denver	16	20	12	4
Cleveland	48	33		25
Newark	33	40	11	
Portland	23	3	20	2
Kansas City	31	15		9
Fort Worth	8	10		
Orlando	36	26		14
Sacramento	22	45		22
Las Vegas	28	18		20
Fort Lauderdale	27	29		
San Francisco	35	43	19	8
San Antonio	25	9		11
San Jose	39	39	5	
Indianapolis	14	16		26
Cincinnati	20	17		34
Norfolk	13	13		19

(cont.)

APPENDIX B *(cont.)*   **The 50 largest metropolitan areas ranked**

City/metropolitan area by population size	*Forbes*: Best Places	Economy.com: Cost of Doing Business	*Expansion Management*: High Value Labor Quotient	BHI: Metro Area Competitive-ness
Charlotte	10	4		16
Columbus	15	22		27
Milwaukee	40	21		18
Bergen-Passaic	43	42	23	
Salt Lake City	29	6		7
Austin	2	12	6	6
New Orleans	45	7		36
Greensboro	37	1		15
Raleigh-Durham	1	2	3	
Nashville	12	5		17
Middlesex	32	41	7	

Note: A blank for *Expansion Management* or BHI indicates that the city was not among the top 50 on that index. The best, lowest cost, or fastest growing city is ranked No. 1.

Source: Author's analysis of indexes.

APPENDIX C
Performance rankings of cities

Four regularly published rankings of cities or metro areas are based solely on measures of economic performance. A brief description of each is included here. Another index that has been cited frequently is "Entrepreneurial Hot Spots," produced by Cognetics Inc. This appears now to be defunct, so we do not include it in our review.[33]

Milken's Best Performing Cities
The Milken Institute, which describes itself as an "independent economic think tank," produces an annual ranking of the 200 largest metropolitan areas in the U.S. on their economic performance (and ranks the 118 smallest metro areas in a separate list). The latest ranking was released in November 2004.

There are nine factors used to rank metro areas. For the first seven, Milken creates an index with the U.S. average equal to 100. The 2004 rankings were based on these components:

1. Five-year job growth: metropolitan area job growth relative to the U.S. average between 1998 and 2003
2. One-year job growth: metropolitan area job growth relative to the U.S. average between 2002 and 2003
3. Five-year wages and salaries growth: salary and wage disbursements growth relative to the U.S. average between 1997 and 2002
4. One-year wages and salaries growth: salary and wage disbursements growth relative to the U.S. average between 2001 and 2002
5. Short-term job growth: job growth/decline between April 2003 and April 2004
6. Five-year relative high-tech GDP growth: high-tech sector output growth relative to the U.S. average between 1998 and 2003
7. One-year relative high-tech GDP growth: high-tech sector output growth relative to the U.S. average between 2002 and 2003
8. 2003 high-tech GDP location quotient: combined metropolitan area high-tech location quotient during 2003. Location quotient (LQ) is a measure of high-tech concentration (U.S. = 1.0). A metro with an LQ higher than 1.0 is said to be more concentrated than the United States and vice versa
9. Number of highly concentrated high-tech industries: measures the number of high-technology industries with a location quotient (LQ) about the U.S. average of 1.0 during 2003

The Milken Institute ranking is a straightforward composite of various measures of economic growth, with a heavy emphasis on growth in high-tech sectors (four of the nine measures being devoted to high tech). The nine measures are combined into an overall index that is the basis for ranking. The Web site does not explain how the measures are combined, though presumably this is contained in the printed report, which can be purchased.

Site Selection*'s Top Metro Areas*

Site Selection magazine has published rankings of U.S. metropolitan areas in the March issue each year since 1991. The March 2004 issue contained rankings of the top 100 metro areas in terms of the number of new or expanded facilities during 2003. The number ranged from nine facilities in each of 12 smaller metro areas to 336 in Chicago. The magazine also listed the top 10 metro areas in terms of total investment, and the 12 states with the most metro areas among the top 100 (presumably in terms of number of facilities, though this is not clear). Since the index measures the total number of facilities or dollars of investment, not a rate (such as dollars per capita), large metro areas and states with more large cities tend to dominate the rankings.

Best Cities for Entrepreneurs

Entrepreneur magazine, in conjunction with Dun and Bradstreet, compiles an annual list of the Best Cities for Entrepreneurs. The ranking is based on four factors:

1. Entrepreneurial activity: number of businesses five years old or younger
2. Small business growth: number of businesses with fewer than 20 employees that experienced "significant employment growth" in the previous year
3. Job growth: "change in job growth [sic] over a three-year period"
4. Risk: bankruptcy rates

The 2003 list (the latest list available on the Web site as of January 2005) included 61 metropolitan areas. There is no explanation of how the scores for each factor are determined or how they are combined into an overall ranking.

Inc.*'s Top Cities for Doing Business*

The latest entrant in the metro-area performance index competition is *Inc.* magazine's Top Cities for Doing Business in America. It ranked 277 cities (actually metropolitan areas) on job growth and sectoral "balance" and published lists of the top 25 in three size categories in the March 2004 issue. More complete results are available on *Inc.*'s Web site.

The overall ranking is based on a combination of its "growth index," weighted about two-thirds, and its "balance index," weighted about one-third. The two indexes for 2004 were each constructed as a weighted average of three measures:

Growth index
1. Current year employment growth (44.4%): three-month rolling averages, from September 2002 through September 2003

2. Capacity to sustain growth (44.4%): 1993-2003 employment growth rate times the ratio of the 1998-2003 growth rate to the 1993-98 growth rate. This in effect measures growth over the past decade, with the latter half of the decade weighted more heavily.
3. Employment momentum (11.1%): difference between current year's growth rate and the average growth rate 2000-03 (September to September). Positive number indicates economy is heating up, negative number means it is slowing down.

Balance index
1. Current sector balance (40%): measures balance among the nine major NAICS industry groups in terms of employment, with the measure "derived from the standard deviation of the employment totals for each major industry group relative to total nonfarm employment"
2. Longer-term balance (40%): measure of balanced growth across a variety of sectors, and "derived from the standard deviation of the percentage contribution of each major NAICS industry group to each region's total 1998-2003 nonfarm employment growth"
3. Recession distortion (20%): "the standard deviation of each sector's recession period growth rate during 2000-03"

The *Inc.* Top Cities ranking is unique among the performance indexes in that it gives weight to balanced growth, rather than simply overall employment growth, though it is not clear from its description exactly how balance is measured. It appears that *Inc.* intends these rankings to be an annual feature of the magazine.

APPENDIX D
Creating an index

Any index must deal with the problem of how to combine disparate measures into a single index number. This involves up to three steps. First, the variables may be ranked, re-scaled, or standardized. Second, the variables may be weighted. Finally, the weighted (or unweighted) variables are added together or averaged to create the index.

Suppose we wish to create an index based on two variables: the amount of the state minimum wage in excess of the federal minimum wage, and the top state corporate income tax rate. The raw measures for three imaginary states are shown in **Table D.1**.

Various possibilities for creating an index based on these two variables are illustrated in **Table D.2**. In all cases, the index authors assume that lower is better on both measures, and the index is constructed such that the state with the lowest index value is "best;" that state receives a ranking of "1" on the overall index.

Index A skips the first two steps, and simply adds the raw variables together. Because the minimum wage varies from 0 to 0.25, while the tax rate varies from 0 to 8, the index is driven almost entirely by the tax rate variable; the minimum wage variable counts for little. To get around this problem, some indexes rank, re-scale, or standardize the measures. These procedures produce a set of variables with similar or identical variability (which may or may not be an improvement).

Index B is constructed by ranking each state (where 1 is "best") on the raw measures and then simply adding the ranks together; the lowest total index score indicates the best overall ranking. Index C is a variant of B; before adding the rankings together, the minimum wage ranking is multiplied by its weight of 3.0 and the tax rate ranking is multiplied by its weight of 1.0.

Index D is an example of re-scaling the variables by assigning the "worst" state on a particular measure a value of 10, the "best" state a value of 0, and pro-rating the remaining states. In this example, State C gets a 6.3 because its tax rate is 63% of the way between the worst and the best. The re-scaled measures are then simply added together; alternatively, they could be weighted and then added.

Index E is an example of standardizing the variables so that they have the same mean and standard deviation. In our example, the raw measures are standardized to a mean of 5.0 and a standard deviation of 1.0. The standardized variables are added together, with or without weighting. (Standardization to a mean of zero and standard deviation of 1 is accomplished by subtracting the mean value of a variable across all states from the value for a particular state, and dividing the result by the standard deviation of that variable; to convert this to a scale with a mean of 5.0 instead of zero, one simply adds 5 to the result.)

APPENDIX TABLE D.1   Raw measures

	State minimum wage above federal	Top rate: state corporate income tax
State A	$0.25	0%
State B	$0.00	8%
State C	$0.25	5%

Source: Author's analysis.

APPENDIX TABLE D.2   Combining raw measures to create an index

	Component measure			
	Minimum wage	Top tax rate	Index	Rank on index
Index A:				
Add raw measures				
State A	0.25	0.0	0.25	1
State B	-	8.0	8.00	3
State C	0.25	5.0	5.25	2
Index B:				
Addrankings of raw measures				
State A	2	1	3	1
State B	1	3	4	2
State C	2	2	4	2
Index C:				
Add weighted rankings				
Weights:	*3.0*	*1.0*		
State A	6	1	7	2
State B	3	3	6	1
State C	6	2	8	3
Index D:				
Add re-scaled measures				
State A	10.0	0.0	10.0	1
State B	0.0	10.0	10.0	1
State C	10.0	6.3	16.3	3
Index E:				
Add standardized measures				
State A	5.7	3.7	9.4	1
State B	3.6	6.1	9.7	2
State C	5.7	5.2	10.9	3

Source: Author's analysis.

Ranking, re-scaling, and standardizing the variables will produce somewhat different rankings from each other, but any of these procedures will reduce the influence of variables with large and varying values compared to variables with small values or values that vary little from one state to another. By standardizing the variables so they have equal means and standard deviations, one ensures that each variable contributes identically to the variation in the overall index score.

Is re-scaling or standardizing necessarily an improvement? Suppose all states have pretty much the same score on a particular measure. One could argue that that measure doesn't really distinguish one state from another and it should not have much influence on the overall index. Standardizing the measure could be seen as artificially creating variation (standard deviation) where little actually exists. However, this is really an empirical question. It is possible that if one is trying to predict growth rates, for example, a measure with large variation will exert little influence on growth rates simply because it is irrelevant, while small differences in another measure will have large effects on growth because that measure is critical to location decisions. Thus in the absence of empirical evidence of the relative importance of different variables, the choice of re-scaling or standardizing procedures is as arbitrary as the choice of weights, since re-scaling or standardizing does in fact change the weight of a given factor. The argument in favor of standardizing is that the weighting is more transparent, since with raw numbers the large variation in influence of various factors will not be at all apparent.

It is possible to create an index using regression analysis. For example, one can estimate an equation predicting differences in state growth rates based on various state characteristics and actual state growth. The resulting equation produces a predicted growth rate for each state based on its characteristics and the estimated coefficients, and these growth rates could simply be divided by the mean growth rate and multiplied by 100. The result is a set of index numbers, where the average state has an index value of 100.

Interestingly, such an index still has problems. When one asks whether a given difference in ranking is statistically significant, the correct answer depends on the significance of the differences in the underlying variables. As a result, the overall index will not necessarily possess the characteristics one would desire. For example, suppose State A and State B have similar index scores that are not significantly different from each other. State C may have a higher score that is significantly different from A but not from B, and D may have a score that is significantly lower than A and B but not C. Even though C is better than A, and A is better than D, one cannot conclude that C is better than D (See Voicu and Lahr 1998).

Endnotes

1. See, for example, CFED (1986) and Atkinson (1990).

2. The latest version of the New Economy Index available on the Internet is for 2002, at www.neweconomyindex.org/states/index.html.

3. Why don't we simply compare the SBSI with data on small business failure or survival rates? Data do exist showing the number of business failures in a given year divided by the number of businesses that existed in the state at the start of the year; this is a failure rate, and one minus that number would be a one-year survival rate. The problem with such data is that the more new businesses that are formed in a state, the more opportunities there are for new businesses to fail, and many fail in the first year or two. Thus high failure rates do not indicate a poor climate for business, but in fact can mean the opposite. In 2003, for example, the employer firm formation rate and the employer firm termination rate were highly correlated (0.74), according to the Small Business Administration's *Small Business Economic Indicators*. (This is why the New Economy Index uses business churning rather than business start-ups as its measure of vitality.)

    We do not have data on true business survival rates by state. This requires the analysis of panel data: we would need to follow a cohort of new businesses for a number of years and determine what percent survive to the third year, the fifth year, the 10th year, etc. One-year survival data of the sort that are available tell us only how many of the firms that existed at the beginning of the year (with ages ranging from 0 to some large number) still existed at the end of the year. There is no way to infer the average life expectancy of a new firm from such data.

4. A correlation coefficient can range in value from -1 to +1. A coefficient of +1 means that, whenever one measure rises by a given percent, the other rises by the same percent. A coefficient of -1 means that whenever one measure rises by a given percent, the other *falls* by the same percent. A value of 0 indicates that the two measures have a completely random relation with one another; when one measure rises, the other is as likely to rise as it is to fall.

5. We also converted the SBSI from an index where lowest is best to one where highest is best by subtracting the SBSI (which ranged from a best of 27 to a worst of 59) from 100, yielding an index that ranged from a best of 73 to a worst of 41. This was necessary since the measures of business vitality are all constructed such that higher is better. The choice of 100 is arbitrary but has no bearing on the results; substitution of any other number would yield identical correlations.

6. The Tax Foundation report also quotes, on p. 15, Helen Ladd's summary of Bartik's 1991 book *Who Benefits From State and Local Economic Development Policies?* to the effect that Bartik "concluded that taxes have quite large and significant effects on business activity." Yet Bartik himself does not actually describe the interstate effects as "quite large" or even "large" in that book, and points out that the tax effects are signifi-

cant only when public services are held constant. In the same book, Bartik argues that tax *increases* could stimulate business activity "if they are used to finance infrastructure and public services used by business" (p. 57). And in a more recent article, Bartik (1994, 853) characterizes the effect of taxes as "modest."

7.   In a box on page 1 of the 2004 report, the foundation says that "this year's study benefited greatly from reactions by government officials and business leaders to the first edition…New sub-indexes capture important tax base issues…."

8.   There are two extreme possibilities, based on the index methodology as described on pages 20 and 34 of the foundation's report. First, if we assume that each of the six components assumes a value from 0 to 1, which appears to be the case from the description, then federal deductibility is just one-third of one-sixth of one-fifth of the base sub-index, or 1.1%. The other extreme possibility consistent with the methodology is that the tax deductibility component actually ranges from 0 to 3, while all others range from 0 to 1, so that federal deductibility is worth 1 point out of 8, in which case it comprises 2.5% of the total base sub-index (one-eighth of one-fifth).

9.   A so-called "jock tax" occurs when the state applies its individual income tax to the income of professional athletes earned while performing in the state. It may apply to visiting entertainers as well.

10.   As with the "potpourri" component of the corporate income tax, the deductibility of federal taxes is either one-third of six variables that range in value from 0 to 1 (and is therefore one-third of one-sixth of one-fourth of the base sub-index, or 1.4%), or it is 1 point out of a total of 8, or 3.1% (one-eighth of one-fourth) of the base sub-index.

11.   The Better Government Association produces an index intended to "describe the extent to which each state has protected itself against possible corruption and made its processes open and accountable to it citizens." It is based on a review of laws regarding freedom of information, whistleblower protection, campaign finance, gifts, and conflicts of interest. See http://www.bettergov.org/pdfs/IntegrityIndex_10.22.02.pdf.

12.   The BHI report attributes this to *Forbes*, but *Forbes*, in turn, used the index created by economy.com.

13.   It is not the average score among all cities in that category, as the four cities with missing data received openness scores ranging from 4.57 to 6.00, nor is it the state score for that category, nor is it the city's average score on the remaining categories.

14.   These figures are from the 2001 version of BHI's state competitiveness index because, in that year, the raw data for each variable for each state were included in the report. In the latest report, we are told only the normalized scores.

15.   We are grateful to the BHI authors for providing a copy of the regression results. They adjusted 2002 and 2003 per capita income first by the national CPI (converting 2002 income to 2003 dollars), and then adjusted each state's 2002 income by the state ACCRA cost-of-living index for the first quarter of 2002, and adjusted each state's 2003 income by the state ACCRA cost-of-living index for the second quarter of 2004. Use of this price index, produced by ACCRA (formerly the American Chamber of Commerce Researchers Association), is highly questionable. Between 2002 and 2004 some of the changes defy common sense: Hawaii's index went from 101.4 to 168.1, California's from 119.7 to 146.1, while Massachusetts' fell from 140 to 125. Overall,

the ACCRA cost of living exhibits a range (from 88 to 168 in 2004, with eight states exceeding 120) far exceeding that of more systematic attempts to construct state cost-of-living indexes, such as those relying on HUD fair market rent data. The latter show a range of about 88 to 112. One of the problems with the ACCRA data is that they are based on surveys conducted in a small number of cities in each state, and the set of cities surveyed can vary from year to year. The state cost of living is an average of the city indexes in each state. This can produce year-to-year variation in the state index that is attributable to changes in the list of component cities, rather than changes in the statewide cost of living. For this reason, ACCRA itself warns that it should not be used to measure inflation from one period to the next. For a more complete discussion of the problems with the ACCRA indexes and the merits of a fair-market-rent index, see Fisher and Gordon (2001, appendix).

16.   This analysis utilized a simple cross-sectional regression with real state per capita income in 2003 (adjusted using the fair-market-rent cost-of-living index) as the dependent variable and the BHI index and real per capita income in 2002 (similarly adjusted) as the explanatory variable. This yielded a very high R2 (0.99), but it was due entirely to the 2002 income variable. Unfortunately, an interstate cost-of-living index was available only for 2001. Thus the analysis adjusts more appropriately for interstate differences in the cost of living due to housing prices and utility rates, but is not able to measure differences across states in the *change* in the cost of living from one year to the next. Still, the results suggest that the BHI results may well be an artifact of the ACCRA cost-of-living index.

17.   A more precise way of getting at the issue of how well the index predicts, and whether its components are measuring factors that really matter, is to replicate BHI's regression analysis, but with each of the eight component scores in the model (as defined in the more logical categories above) instead of just the overall index. This was done for three years: 2001, 2002, and 2003 (unadjusted for interstate cost-of-living differences). The results do not provide much support for the index factors. By far the most significant determinant in all three years was the previous year's income level. The coefficients were significant at the 1% level and had values near 1, meaning that a $1,000 difference between two states in 2002 income, for example, would predict about a $1,000 difference in incomes between the two states in 2003. While five of the eight components were statistically significant in the 2003 model, three had the wrong sign. In the 2002 model, none of those five were significant, but two others were. In the 2001 model, only the "other" variable was statistically significant. In a model predicting growth in per capita income from 1999 to 2003, only the "other" variable was significant. This is ironic, since this is the only one of the eight components that has no real meaning; it is where we dumped the variables that didn't really belong in any measure of either climate or outcomes. Leaving the "other" component out of the model did not improve the significance of any of the other components, however, except for the amenities measure, which was positive and significant at the 1% level.

18.   In the text, this variable is described as "tax revenue" only, while in the appendix table, it is described as "own-source general revenue," which would include such things as charges for services and interest, in addition to taxes.

19.   See previous note.

20. Neither the Cato Institute nor the author, Stephen Moore, responded to inquiries as to the identity of the states, nor did they reply when asked if the comparisons in Table 4 of the report were based on an earlier study by Stephen Moore of 10 tax-cutting and tax-raising states.

21. This report was distributed by the American Legislative Exchange Council as the October 2002 issue of their policy periodical "The State Factor," and is available on the ALEC Web site.

22. Following the Cato method, we converted the average annual percent changes in per capita spending and revenue, and in spending and revenue per $1,000 of personal income, to index numbers, with the largest increase given a value of 0 and the smallest increase (or largest decline) a value of 100. We also included the 2000 tax rate variable (the sum of the top income tax rates, converted to an index), and then averaged the five to produce a composite score, which varied from 18 to 89.

23. The analysis produced a low $R2$ (0.19), with per capita income in 1994 negative and statistically significant. Neither a composite index of spending and revenue changes nor the top corporate/individual income tax rate (converted to an index) were close to statistical significance at the 10% level.

24. Inquiries to Global Economic Software, producers of the CD with the raw data that are behind the index, were forwarded to the author of the analysis, Professor Bobby McCormick of Clemson University. He did not reply to this or to follow-up inquiries asking for the calculations that produce the index numbers from the raw data.

25. The way in which these 47 rankings were constructed is described in an appendix in the book. However, using the raw variables from the dataset and following the procedures as described in the appendix, we were unable to reproduce the scores for any of the sectors, though we came close. In part this is due to some differences between the variables listed in the appendix and those in the database.

26. Vermont gets a boost on this index by being the only state with a sales tax that exempts restaurant meals.

27. The migration data is apparently from the 2000 Census, which asks people to identify where they lived five years previous. That the data refer to 1995-2000 migration is clear from the database, though it is not specified in the published report.

28. There is one other ranking that could be construed as a competitiveness index: *Expansion Management*'s "Fifty Hottest Cities." This ranking is unique in that it is based on an annual survey of site selection consultants to find out "which cities their clients find most attractive." The most recent survey (the seventh) appeared in the January 2005 issue of *Expansion Magazine*. The magazine surveyed over 80 consultants, asking them to "list their top city choices for relocating and expanding manufacturing companies, taking into consideration such factors as the business climate, work force quality, operating costs, incentive programs, and the ease of working with local political and economic development officials." There is no other information given regarding the survey methodology; all that is reported is the ranking. One is left to assume that the overall rank for a given city is the average of the rankings of that city by all the respondents. There is no objective or quantifiable information underlying this index, and one has to wonder how much thought the average consultant puts into the responses, and how idiosyncratic the rankings may be, dependent as they are on recent experiences of a non-random sample of consultants.

29. Email correspondence from Kurt Rankin, March 3, 2005.

30. In the report, the exact measure is variously described as "labor compensation per dollar of output," "relative earnings/productivity," output (gross product) per worker, or earnings per worker. It may be that earnings per worker (compensation rate) is divided by output per worker (productivity) to arrive at earnings per dollar of output, but this is not clear.

31. Conversation with Senior Editor Kurt Badenhausen of *Forbes*, March 4, 2005. The magazine does not divulge the exact weights employed.

32. When asked of the usefulness of the Grant Thornton Index in making location decisions, the head of General Motors' location office said they are of little use, GM performing its own analysis for every project, emphasizing access to markets and suppliers (which cannot really be incorporated into a statewide, generic business climate.) See Atkinson 1990.

33. Cognetics, an economic consulting firm in Waltham, Mass. founded by David Birch, at one time produced a list titled "Entrepreneurial Hot Spots: The Best Places in America to Start and Grow a Company." This was a pure performance index. States and metro areas were ranked according to two measures: (1) significant starts: local businesses started in the past 10 years and employing at least five people, as a percent of all companies; and (2) young growers: local businesses that were 10 years old or less four years ago and that had a "growth index" of at least 3 over the past four years, as a percent of all companies. The growth index is the company's percentage employment growth times its absolute employment growth (to avoid biasing the growth measure in favor of the largest or smallest companies). An overall index was created as a weighted average of the two measures. The Cognetics rankings were used by Inc.com, the Web version of *Inc.* magazine, to create *Inc.*'s Best Cities lists in December 2000. Cognetics released a 2001 Entrepreneurial Hot Spots report in July 2002, and it was reported on at Microsoft's bCentral.com. A search of the web did not reveal any more recent references; both the ranking and Cognetics appear to be defunct. The only "Cognetics" currently on the Web is Cognetics Corporation in Princeton, N.J., which does not appear to have any relation to David Birch's firm. An online yellow pages directory lists "Arc Analytics (formerly Cognetics Inc.)" at the Cognetics Inc. address and phone number in Waltham, Mass. No one answers the phone.

References

Atkinson, Robert. 1990. "Understanding Business Climate Studies: Their Use and Validity." *Economic Development Review*, Winter, pp. 46-49.

Bartik, Timothy J. 1991. *Who Benefits From State and Local Economic Development Policies?* Kalamazoo, Mich.: W.E. Upjohn Institute for Employment Research.

Bartik, Timothy J. 1994. "Jobs, Productivity and Local Economic Development: What Implications Does Economic Research Have for the Role of Government?" *National Tax Journal* 47(4).

Beacon Hill Institute (BHI). 2004. *Metro Area and State Competitiveness Report, 2004.* Boston, Mass.: Suffolk University. Available at: http://www.beaconhill.org/.

Cato Institute. 2005. *Fiscal Policy Report Card on America's Governors: 2002.* By Stephen Moore and Steven Slivinski. Washington, D.C.: Cato Institute. Available at: http://www.cato.org/pub_display.php?pub_id=1313.

Corporation for Enterprise Development. 1986. *Taken for Granted: How Grant Thornton's Business Climate Index Leads States Astray.* Washington, D.C.: CFED.

Ditsler, Elaine, and Peter Fisher. 2003. *Taxes and State Economic Growth: The Myths and the Reality.* Policy Brief. Mt. Vernon, Iowa: The Iowa Policy Project.

Economy.com. "Cost of Doing Business Index." West Chester, Pa.: economy.com. Available at: http://www.economy.com/store/single_product.asp?pid=11-00001-01. (Copy of the 2002 State Cost of Business Index available on the Web site of the Public Policy Institute of New York: http://www.ppinys.org/reports/jtf2004/relativecost.htm. A good description of the metropolitan area index can be found at: http://regional-institute.buffalo.edu/sotr/00/1_econ/1_4.html. The actual index for each metro area can be found as part of the *Forbes* Best Cities ranking.)

Entrepreneur Magazine. "Best Cites for Entrepreneurs." Available at: http://www.entrepreneur.com/bestcities/0,5271,,00.html.

Expansion Management. "State, Metro and School District Quotients." Available at: http://www.expansionmanagement.com/.

Expansion Management. "50 Hottest Cities, 2005." Available at: http://www.expansionmanagement.com/smo/articleviewer/default.asp?cmd=articledetail&articleid=16323&st=5.

Fisher, Peter, and Colin Gordon. 2001. *The State of Working Iowa, 2001.* Mt. Vernon, Iowa: The Iowa Policy Project.

Forbes Magazine. "Best Places." Available at: http://www.forbes.com/2004/05/05/04bestplacesland.html.

Goetz, Stephen, and David Freshwater. 2001. "State Level Determinants of Entrepreneurship and a Preliminary Measure of Entrepreneurial Climate." *Economic Development Quarterly* 15(1): 58-70.

Heald, Brian. 2003. "Redefining Business Success: Distinguishing Between Closure and Failure." *Small Business Economics* 21: 51-61.

Inc. Magazine. "Top 25 Cities for Doing Business in America." Available at: http://www.inc.com/magazine/20040301/top25.html.

Lawton, Charles, and Frank O'Hara. 2004. *Ranking Maine's Economic Climate.* Augusta, Maine: Maine Center for Economic Policy.

Lynch, Robert G. 2004. *Rethinking Growth Strategies: How State and Local Taxes and Services Affect Economic Development.* Washington, D.C.: Economic Policy Institute.

Milken Institute. "Best Performing Cities." Available at http://www.milkeninstitute.org/index.taf.

Orszag, Peter, and Joseph Stiglitz. 2001. "Budget Cuts Versus Tax Increases at the State Level: Is One More Counter-Productive Than the Other During a Recession?" Washington, D.C.: Center on Budget and Policy Priorities.

Pacific Research Institute (PRI). 2004. *U.S. Economic Freedom Index, 2004 Report.* By Ying Huan, Robert E. McCormick, and Lawrence J. McQuillan. San Francisco, Calif: PRI. Available at: http://www.pacificresearch.org/centers/cfe/index.html.

Peters, Alan, and Peter Fisher. 2002. *State Enterprise Zone Programs: Have They Worked?* Kalamazoo, Mich.: W.E. Upjohn Institute for Employment Research.

Popkin, Joel. 1991. "Business Survival Rates by Age Cohort of Business." Washington, D.C.: U.S. Small Business Administration, RS Number 122.

Progressive Policy Institute. 2002. *The New Economy Index.* Avaliable at: www.neweconomyindex.org/states/index.html.

Sims, Richard. 2003. "A Grain of Salt: A Critical Review of the Beacon Hill Institute's State Competitiveness Report." Washington, D.C.: Institute on Taxation and Economic Policy.

Site Selection Magazine. "Top Metro Areas." Available at http://www.siteselection.com/ (March issue).

Skoro, Charles. 1988. "Rankings of State Business Climates: An Evaluation of Their Usefulness in Forecasting." *Economic Development Quarterly* 2(2): 138-152.

Small Business and Entrepreneurship Council. 2004. *Small Business Survival Index 2004: Ranking the Policy Environment for Entrepreneurship Across The Nation.* By Raymond J. Keating. Washington, D.C.: SBEC. Available at: http://www.sbsc.org/Media/pdf/SBSI_2004.pdf.

Tannenwald, Robert. 2004. *Massachusetts Business Taxes: Unfair? Inadequate? Uncompetitive?* Boston, Mass.: Federal Reserve Bank of Boston, Discussion Paper No. 04-4.

Tannenwald, Robert. 1996. "Business Tax Climate: How Should It Be Measured and How Important Is It?" *State Tax Notes*, May 13, pp. 1459-1471.

Tax Foundation. 2004. *State Business Tax Climate Index*. By Scott A. Hodge, J. Scott Moody, and Wendy P.Warcholik. Background Paper. Washington, D.C.: Tax Foundation. Available at: http://www.taxfoundation.org/sbtci.html.

U.S. Small Business Administration. 2004a. Database downloaded from the SBA Office of Advocacy web site: http://www.sba.gov/advo/research/dyn_st_98_02n1.txt

U.S. Small Business Administration. 2004b. *Small Business Economic Indicators for 2003*. Washington, D.C.: SBA, Office of Advocacy.

Voicu, Alexandru, and Michael Lahr. 1998. "Creating a Cost-of-Doing Business Index." Mimeo. New Brunswick, N.J.: Rutgers University.

Wasylenko, Michael. 1997. "Taxation and Economic Development: The State of the Literature." *New England Economic Review* (Federal Reserve Bank of Boston), March/April, pp. 37-52.

Zahradnik, Robert. 2005. "Tax Cuts and Consequences: The States That Cut Taxes the Most During the 1990s Have Suffered Lately." Washington, D.C.: Center on Budget and Policy Priorities.

About EPI

The Economic Policy Institute was founded in 1986 to widen the debate about policies to achieve healthy economic growth, prosperity, and opportunity.

In the United States today, inequality in wealth, wages, and income remains historically high. Expanding global competition, changes in the nature of work, and rapid technological advances are altering economic reality. Yet many of our policies, attitudes, and institutions are based on assumptions that no longer reflect real world conditions.

With the support of leaders from labor, business, and the foundation world, the Institute has sponsored research and public discussion of a wide variety of topics: trade and fiscal policies; trends in wages, incomes, and prices; education; the causes of the productivity slowdown; labor market problems; rural and urban policies; inflation; state-level economic development strategies; comparative international economic performance; and studies of the overall health of the U.S. manufacturing sector and of specific key industries.

The Institute works with a growing network of innovative economists and other social science researchers in universities and research centers in the U.S. and abroad who are willing to go beyond the conventional wisdom in considering strategies for public policy.

Founding scholars of the Institute include Jeff Faux, distinguished fellow and former president of EPI; Lester Thurow, Sloan School of Management, MIT; Ray Marshall, former U.S. secretary of labor, professor at the LBJ School of Public Affairs, University of Texas; Barry Bluestone, Northeastern University; Robert Reich, former U.S. secretary of labor; and Robert Kuttner, author, editor of *The American Prospect,* and columnist for *Business Week* and the Washington Post Writers Group.

For additional information about the Institute, contact EPI at 1660 L Street NW, Suite 1200, Washington, DC 20036, (202) 775-8810, or visit www.epinet.org.